Social Enterprise Unraveled

WILLEMIJN VERLOOP
MARK HILLEN

SOCIAL ENTERPRISE UNRAVELED

Best practice from the Netherlands

Warden Press

© 2014 Willemijn Verloop and Mark Hillen

ISBN paperback: 978-94-92004-02-4
ISBN e-book (Epub): 978-94-92004-05-5
ISBN e-book (Mobi/Kindle): 978-94-92004-06-2

Original title: *Verbeter de wereld, begin een bedrijf.*
Hoe social enterprises winst voor iedereen creëren
Amsterdam: Business Contact, 2013
This edition published by Warden Press/Wardy Poelstra,
Amsterdam
Translated from the Dutch by Erwin Postma, Malaga
Cover design: Simons & Boom, Arnhem
Cover image: Pearson + Maron
Photo authors: Erik Smits, Amsterdam
Interior design/lay-out: Sander Pinkse Boekproducties,
Amsterdam

'I believe that social business is key to a more sustainable, responsible, and more inclusive future for Europe.'

José Manuel Durão Barroso, President of the European Commission

Cases

Table of contents

Businesses changing the world

The concept of social enterprise as a distinct type of
business is very valuable.

Social enterprises are truly different from other businesses, and deserve recognition and acclaim. Their aim
is primarily societal and they can therefore create great
value for humankind. Social enterprises are ideal vehicles
to help solve social problems as pioneers and as shining
examples.

The social enterprise sector is still young and developing. The interpretation of what a social enterprise is, and
what it is not, differs across the globe. But we are seeing
the commonality between definitions grow, as social
enterprises are ever more clearly set apart from charities,
commercial enterprises, and public sector organizations.
While the definition of a social enterprise is coming
together, the inner workings of a social enterprise and the
impact of its services will continue to be determined by
three factors that differ from one country to the next. First,
a social enterprise is primarily aimed at solving societal challenges, which can differ by region, country, and
community, giving rise to different social missions and
services. The role that the government plays is the second
factor that sets the playing field for social enterprises.
Within the boundaries of legislation and regulations,

social enterprises fill the gaps left by public services. And, last but not least, the way people choose to work together is culturally bound and reflected in how social enterprises operate.

This book is about the emerging social enterprise sector in the Netherlands, our home country. Our book contains our viewpoints, strongly bedded in the policies of the European Commisison, and cases of Dutch social enterprises. Many of these examples can be found in other countries, but some are rather specific to the Netherlands. In any case, it will be of interest to the international reader to compare and reflect. And so we hope to contribute to the development of the social enterprise sector across the globe.

The Netherlands needs a strong sector dedicated to social entrepreneurship. Although the Netherlands is among the world's ten richest countries, it is by no means problem-free. Numerous social issues have yet to be tackled. There are over one million Dutch people who live below the poverty line and two million Dutch people who are considered to be lonely. We believe loneliness is also a form of poverty, a psychological and extremely distressing form of poverty. Another problem that exists in the Netherlands is that 27,000 young people drop out of senior vocational education every year. This is not only a problem for themselves, but also for the rest of society. Keeping young people in school helps prevent them from causing problems and instead contribute to the economy and society. Jumping to the environment, 4 percent of the Netherlands' energy comes from alternative sources, which is low compared to Germany, where 25 percent is produced from renewable sources.

Amsterdam and Rotterdam, the Netherlands' main cities, are not able to adhere to the minimum European Union air quality standard. Inhabitants of these cities are 20 percent more likely to get lung cancer than people living in rural areas. The social enterprise business model is ideally suited to help solve these types of problems. In addition, a large number of social enterprises focus on solving poverty in developing countries, which can be done through fair trade or through establishing social businesses there.

There is still so much left to do. Social entrepreneurs are coming up with effective and sustainable solutions. By setting up companies with actual impact, companies that connect people, create jobs for disabled people, and propose solutions to environmental issues.

This book describes the phenomenon of a social enterprise, highlighting its social and human value and why it is a special and unusual form of business. We will also show how they come about and what challenges they face, because when starting a social enterprise, an entrepreneur is not choosing the path of least resistance.

We hope this book will enlighten and inspire, and energize you in the way social entrepreneurs have energized us. Get governments to create better conditions and opportunities, in a facilitating rather than a subsidizing role. Spur on investors to put their money into social enterprises. Induce universities to do more research and teaching on social entrepreneurship, thus producing large crops of talented social business students. But there is still plenty left to do. And everyone can do something, which is the great thing about social enterprise. We hope reading this book will inspire everyone, regardless of their role — as a consumer, policymaker, commissioning party, financial backer — to help make this industry successful.

The first chapter will describe social enterprise, its defining features, what social enterprises are, and why they are truly different: the new exceptional combination of idealism and business. Chapter 2 will subsequently go into the figure of the social entrepreneur: what drives him or her, what are some of the personal traits of someone who chooses to become a social entrepreneur? Chapter 3 deals with the social enterprise business model: the value a social enterprise seeks to create goes far beyond mere financial profit. Chapter 4 is about social enterprises, which like any other business have to attract and retain customers, position and sell their product or service, and will answer the question what you can and cannot do with your underlying idealism. Chapter 5 delves into the concepts of community interest and involvement, also covering citizen initiatives and value created for the community. Chapter 6 explains how to quantify social impact. Chapter 7 describes the inner workings of a social enterprise, its DNA, its nature, which inherently ensues from its social vigor, the fact that all stakeholders have a say, the ethics, and transparency. In Chapter 8, the focus shifts to how social enterprises are funded and which issues arise in that context. Chapter 9 centers on relations between social enterprises and the government. Chapter 10 will conclude with a look at the future of social enterprise, asking where social enterpreneurship is headed, and what it needs.

We hope you enjoy reading this book and that it will inspire you to actively support the development of social entrepreneurship — or even to become a social entrepreneur yourself!

Source citations and references to relevant books and articles are available online on www.social-enterprise.nl/book. On this same website, you can also submit any questions you have after reading this book.

Taxi Electric: quadruple impact

Our first case is Amsterdam's Taxi Electric, a young company that has managed to have a societal impact on as many as four fronts. Taxi Electric was established in 2011 by Edvard Hendriksen and Ruud Zandvliet, two young economists who could no longer bear to see how we are treating our living environment. They quit their jobs at a major corporation and started Taxi Electric.

Taxi Electric's quadruple impact starts with the environment, as their fleet of taxis is exclusively made up of eco-friendly Nissan Leafs — fully electric zero-emission vehicles. That in itself is already a major gain, because regular taxis are extreme polluters, at least thirty-five percent more so than regular cars. Amsterdam has poor air quality, and the city will fail to meet European air quality standards by 2015, with one of the measures being to have at least 450 zero-emission cabs by then. Ruud and Edvard's aim is to run one hundred of them. By so doing, they are showing that exploiting electric cabs and making a profit is possible. If they pull that off, others will follow their example and help Amsterdam reach its target. "It's also about scale," says Ruud. "You cannot make a profit with ten vehicles, and with thirty to forty you will only break even, but one hundred will generate a turnover of 10 million euros and get you a reasonable margin." Taxi Electric is in no way subsidized, it is primarily funded by private investors.

But Ruud and Edvard have taken their social entrepreneurship further by also helping to make the world a better place through their employment policy: nearly all their drivers are over fifty and returning to paid work after a long period of unemployment, which is a demographic in the Netherlands that struggles to get back to work without a little extra help. This employment opportunity not only benefits their drivers, but also the company itself: the drivers are nice and polite people, who look tidy and open the door for you, because that is part of the Taxi Electric service. "We also want to offer good value for money, which is not always easy to find in Amsterdam," Ruud says subtly.

With their good manners, which should in fact be common practice, Taxi Electric is helping to improve the Amsterdam cab industry's lousy public image. This is the third area where the company is having an impact. And this just happens to be an area where there is a lot of ground to be made up in Amsterdam!

And fourthly, and perhaps most importantly in the long term, the company is helping to boost the uptake of electric vehicles. Unknown, unloved: electric vehicles do not have a great public image yet. In a Taxi Electric cab, customers get a first-hand experience of the fact that electric cars pull away quicker than gasoline-driven ones and can easily hit 130 km/h on the interstate. "Ours are the fastest cabs in town," says Ruud. Their drivers can explain exactly how much range their cab has, or how the battery charges itself during braking, and that it now only takes under thirty minutes to charge the battery. This effectively makes a ride in one of Edvard and Ruud's cabs a test drive in an electric vehicle. This is a company that sets the right example, achieving a quadruple impact.

The reasonable man adapts himself to the world; the unreasonable one persists in trying to adapt the world to himself. Therefore all progress depends on the unreasonable man.

George Bernard Shaw, *Man and Superman* (1903)

1

Business-minded idealists

What are social enterprises — and what are they not?

There are many different ways to start a business. You may have mastered a trade, let's say that of shoemaker, and you hire an apprentice — first only one but you keep hiring more and more. That's how Gucci and Adidas, for example, started. Or a couple of employees who launch a corporate spin-off, thinking they can do better than the company they used to work for. Or two socially engaged boys who don't know what to do with their lives and spend their last two dollars on getting an ice cream-making diploma — that's the story behind Ben & Jerry's. Also possible.

Every entrepreneur has a different reason to start a business, and it is generally a combination of several motives: the founder has spotted a gap in the market or wants to use his or her talents, do what he or she is good at and likes doing. Or he or she wants to show the world what he or she can do. The primary motive is often the need to earn a living, and starting a business seems like the best way of doing that.

But you can also be driven to start a business to better the world. You have identified a social problem and think your business idea can help solve that problem, like our friends at Taxi Electric. Odd? Unusual? Maybe so in the present day and age, but increasingly less so: over the past few decades, entrepreneurs have cropped up all over the world whose main aim was to better the world.

A social enterprise:

1. primarily has a social mission: impact first
2. realizes that mission as an independent enterprise that provides a service or product
3. is financially self-sustaining, based on trade or other forms of value exchange, and therefore barely, if at all, dependent on donations or subsidies
4. is social in the way it is governed:
   - a social enterprise is transparent
   - profits are allowed, but financial targets are subordinate to the mission, shareholders get a reasonable slice of profits
   - all stakeholders have a balanced say in strategy and management
   - a social enterprise is fair to everyone
   - a social enterprise is aware of its ecological footprint.

Their companies are called social enterprises. The most famous, and perhaps even the mother of all social enterprises, is Grameen Bank, which was founded by Muhammad Yunus in Bangladesh in 1976. Yunus believed the best way to fight poverty was not through charity, but by enabling people to help themselves. And so he started giving small loans to the poor, to women in particular, who had no access to funding until then. By now, Grameen Bank has issued over 13 billion dollars in microcredit loans, but even more importantly: the concept of microfinance has taken off on a global scale. When Grameen Bank's business model turned out to work, social entrepreneurs in other poor countries launched similar initiatives. Regular commercial enterprises have since also entered the microcredit business, which has meanwhile grown into an 80-billion-dollar industry. This development has helped 200 million poor people, the so-called bottom of the pyramid, gain access to financial services. In 2006, Yunus was awarded the Nobel Peace Prize, making him the only entrepreneur to ever receive this prize.

Social enterprises come in all shapes and sizes. Some focus on energy, others on fair food, and yet others on people who, for whatever reason, are unable to hold down a job without special attention and support. There are major ones, virtually multinationals, and small ones, operated from an attic somewhere. And as you would expect from a young industry: not everyone everywhere in the world goes by the same definition of what a social enterprise is and what it is not. For the sake of clarity, we will present our definitions in this chapter, which largely follow those used by the European Union.

Financially self-sustaining

Social enterprises are organizations with the same objectives as charities, but operate based on the principles of the private sector, which includes the need to grow and ability to realize reasonable financial returns. A social enterprise is just like any other company: the company provides a product or service and has a revenue model. That said, making money is not the main aim, but rather a means to an end, with the end being to achieve social impact.

An organization that runs on donations or subsidies is not a business. If you are largely dependent on donations, you are a charity. If your organization relies heavily on taxpayers' money, you are part of the public sector, and therefore not a company. But when is an organization a social enterprise?

According to Wikipedia, corporate social responsibility (CSR), sustainable responsible business, or social performance is focused on economic performance (profit), while respecting the social side (people) and operating within eco-friendly conditions (planet). Many commercial companies — perhaps even most of them — play an important role in society: they make medication for our health, responsibly produce the food we need to live, or develop and build solar panels and electric vehicles. By far most commercial enterprises are increasingly aware of their responsibility, and this awareness is translating itself into highly concrete programs. Not only by sustainable operations "on the fringe" (do no harm), but also more and more in their core business. Still, this does not make these companies social enterprises, as their financial objective takes precedence over their social objective. This difference may seem subtle, but does indeed show in the company's behavior. These companies will always pursue high financial targets, which exclude certain services and innovations.

And in many cases, the decision to adopt CSR is not driven by social or ethical motives, by a will to do good, but rather by financial objectives in various ways. It looks good to the outside world and is helpful in a company's human resources policy. Young people want to work at social and eco-friendly companies. CSR helps companies attract the best people. The most direct financial interest lies in the relation with investors. A high listing on the Dow Jones Sustainability Index will make a company's share price shoot up.

Needless to say, this is not an exact science. We use 75 percent as a guideline: when an organization generates over 75 percent of its revenue through trading products or services we consider it a social enterprise. Otherwise, we consider it a charity or public sector organization. A social enterprise may therefore obtain part of its income from subsidies, donations, or, for example, voluntary work, which often actually turns out to be the only way a social enterprise can survive in the early years of its existence. But at the end of the day, a social enterprise is an independently operating company that can support itself financially through trading.

Social value								Financial value
Charities/Public sector		Social enterprise				Traditional business		
Grants or subsidies only, no trading	Grants or subsidies and trading	Potentially sustainable >75% trading revenue	Break even all income from trading	Profit surplus reinvested	Profit distribution socially driven	CSR company	Company allocating percentage to charity	Main-stream market company
Impact only			*Impact first*				*Finance first*	

The social enterprise focuses on impact first. Source: Venturesome, Shaerpa.

Different from CSR

There is a great difference between social enterprises and traditional businesses that assume their corporate social responsibility. These latter companies go to great lengths to operate in a way that minimizes the negative impact on society, trying even to ensure that people and planet benefit. But no matter how admirable and useful that is, such companies were not founded with the objective of creating social value in mind. Although, for example, Ahold, the largest supermarket chain in the Netherlands, looks for ways of cutting their carbon emissions, makes an effort to get more organic and fair trade products on their shelves, and seeks to employ disabled people, it never ceases to be a company that is run based on financial value. Ahold's share price features prominently on their website, and the "results" section lists only financial parameters. There is nothing wrong with that, as it instantly tells us where Ahold's priorities lie. When push comes to shove, people and planet will take a backseat to shareholder

value. Regardless of how important their stores are in the community and how much people at Ahold are genuinely trying to do things better. Corporate social responsibility is a side show, while social entrepreneurship is a primary objective.

Social

As mentioned above, there are many organizations that "do good," but when do their actions become truly "social?" In the following, we will present our take on the most important social objectives.

- **Well-being**, and then in particular for the underprivileged and the disadvantaged. They need special attention to be able to exercise their basic human rights, although it would be even better to go one step further, to lift them out of marginalization and empower them to take part in society through employment and an income.
- **Social wealth and cohesion**. The idea is to forge contact between people, often within local communities, which is an elementary human need. New contacts lead to new commitment that can be centered on the other two objectives listed here, caring for each other and for the environment. Ethical conduct, meaning the way people associate with each other, also falls within this category of objectives.

- **Ecology**. Major issues such as global warming and declining biodiversity are shouting out for solutions. Everywhere mankind is faced with environmental problems caused by population density, clogged roads, and intensive agriculture. Social enterprises are often ecological pioneers that work on sustainable development, clean energy, healthy food, and smart mobility.

The word "social" refers to the interests of a greater unit, a community, a country, or the world as a whole. Besides directly involved shareholders, employees, or paying customers, a social enterprise has more beneficiaries. When you ride a Taxi Electric cab instead of a diesel-powered one, residents of the neighborhoods you're passing through will all benefit, because the air they breathe is just a little bit cleaner and healthier thanks to you.

Marqt: stop talking and do something

Working at Ahold supermarkets, Quirijn Bolle learned about the ins and outs of the food industry. He saw healthy products that were kept out of the chain, while unnecessary (and harmful) substances were added to the majority of the supermarket chain's assortment. At one point, he said to himself: this has to change. For what are we as a society doing if this is how we organize our food industry? In his view, the industry was morally bankrupt, but the world just hadn't cottoned on to that yet. Quirijn: "The horse has bolted, but the machine just keeps going. The other day, I spoke to a supermarket manager with a turnover of 7.5 million euros a year. But he doesn't make a profit, as margins have dropped to such a low level that he can't even break even. And then you're only talking about the supermarket, most of which manage to eke out a tiny margin at least, and not about the producers, who have their backs against the wall, and not about the animals that are kept in dismal conditions. What on earth are we doing?'

Bolle decided to have a go at turning the entire industry upside down by opening a fair food store: Marqt. Marqt serves an important social purpose: in the area of consumers' health, farmers' livelihoods, animal welfare, employment, the positive effect on the street scene, stores' energy efficiency, less transport, and so on.

There were setbacks aplenty at the start and as the enterprise grew, pushing Quirijn's venture dangerously close to the brink of failure on several occasions. Never daunted by these setbacks, Quirijn always held his conviction that he would succeed. 'I really know from the tips of my toes that things should be done differently. And seeing as this belief comes from the tip of my toes, I have to be the one to do it. Because if I don't, who will? There is so much talk, but I say: stop talking, and do something. What do I have to lose? And it also gives me tremendous energy.'

Bringing about real change

Social enterprises have different kinds of impact and contribute to social innovation. The most ambitious entrepreneur wants to solve a certain social problem once and for all — that is the ideal. We call that aiming for systemic change: "the system" will then have been changed to such a degree that the problem has actually disappeared. But there are also numerous social entrepreneurs who pursue smaller goals and, for example, seek to bring about real change for a small community, which is equally commendable.

Impact can occur on three levels:
1. locally
2. through a step change
3. systemic change

A social enterprise can have major impact on a community or a small group, but may lack the capacity or mission to have an impact on a larger scale. One fine example of this is that of a restaurant called Fifteen, which gives disadvantaged youngsters work experience and training (see page 55). The effect may be confined to the youngsters and the restaurant, but means a great deal to the people who work there and their future prospects, moving on to normal jobs when they are able to.

   Social enterprises that have the kind of clout that enables them to generate greater impact create a step change. This is what happens when, for example, companies manage to reach far greater numbers of people they can help. This is possible when a company succeeds in acquiring sufficient means to roll their service or product out on a larger scale. Growth in scale not only comes with growth of the social enterprise itself, it is also a result of other companies following suit by copying the concept. This happens when an entrepreneur is successful, when the impact is great, and the company has a clean bill of financial health. That is when the venture achieves credibility, inspiring others and paving the way for the next stage. Things snowball into "a step change." Taxi Electric may not have the potential to solve air pollution, it can make a big contribution.

But how you do get from there to systemic change? Well, system change is achieved when an entire "industry" is created, which covers such a large scale that the existing problem disappears slowly but surely. Scaling up a social enterprise and others following suit are key prerequisites for system change, but that is not enough. For true system change, people's hearts and minds must be won. It requires broad acceptance and recognition that the social problem is a pressing one and that a solution is available. Only then will large numbers of people and organizations back the initiative and generate the kind of mass support that will lead to a lasting change to the system.

We have already mentioned Grameen Bank and the Nobel Prize. Microcredit has meanwhile become a true system in its own right, an industry that moves 80 billion dollars and functions "as a system" that has lifted hundreds of millions of people out of poverty. Max Havelaar, the first ever fair trade label, also falls into this category: thirty years after its founding, supermarket shelves feature ever more fair trade products, which is having a positive impact on the lives of the farmers that produce them. Tony's Chocolonely has raised the bar even higher with its concept of "slavery-free," aiming for an even broader system change that would see all cocoa farmers lifted above the poverty line and allow them to send their children to school instead of to work. And not only those farmers who supply to Tony's Chocolonely, but all farmers, by mobilizing consumers, setting the right example, and directly influencing other players in the industry to do more.

Fairphone is a social enterprise that seeks to unleash a revolution in the electronics industry in a similar manner, by marketing the world's first fair cell phones and purging the chain from top to bottom. Fairphone offers socially conscious consumers an alternative and leads by example. That is what system change looks like, and this is the role of social enterprise in the integrated solution of a social issue.

An entrepreneur who pursues system change will get on his or her soapbox to inspire others to follow suit, calling for competitors, which is the precise opposite of what a commercial entrepreneur would do. And this is what we have seen nearly every single entrepreneur covered in this book do.

Ctaste: success in the dark

Diners doing the conga in the restaurant, the waiter in front, diners behind with a hand on the shoulder of the person before, where do you get that? At the end of a night of heavy drinking? During carnival? No, it's actually a daily occurrence at Amsterdam's Ctaste restaurant. The lights in the dining area are off, and stay off, because this is a dining-in-the-dark experience. Waiters and other staff are never inconvenienced by this: they are visually impaired. "Experts in the dark," says Sandra Ballij (31), who founded and runs Ctaste together with her husband. Back when she still worked at ING Bank, she found herself one day, by pure coincidence, dining in the dark at Dans le Noir restaurant in Paris. It turned into a fascinating experience, and that same night she asked her boyfriend (now husband): "Why don't we open a restaurant like this?" The idea tied in with her true passion of starting a business, and so they decided to import the concept to the Netherlands. And it caught on, after its opening in 2007, the restaurant has had around 100,000 guests conga into its dining area, and it is making a profit. Things are going so well that they have already paid off the 50,000 euro start-up loan from the Start Foundation, which subsequently refunded all interest Ctaste had paid: "Ctaste is a real gem in our portfolio of social entrepreneurs."

"With this company, my intention was to give people who are normally sidelined in society a chance to get involved," Ballij explains. "Being out of work makes you passive, perhaps even depressed. And blind and visually impaired people also hear the following words far too often: let me do that for you. Society makes them passive, albeit with the best of intentions. It is so great to see how proud our employees are of their job, of what they can actually do, of the fact that they are earning a living. From the moment they walk in here, you can see them grow, see their insecurity decrease and their self-esteem increase. Isn't that fantastic?"

And yet, Ctaste met with quite a lot of skepticism at first, also from rather unexpected circles, including the interest group for the blind and visually impaired, which — out of a misplaced sense of wanting to protect — advised its members not to get a job so as not to jeopardize their welfare entitlements. "But what is wrong with turning a full-time welfare recipient into a full-time waiter?" Ballij counters. And funnily enough, it actually turned out to be quite difficult to find visually impaired staff. The Dutch employee insurance and welfare administration (UWV) does not keep records of jobseekers' impairments, because that is considered discrimination. "That's not how it should be," says Ballij, "that information should be included in their files. I believe that everybody, including people with a disability, can be good at something. Look at people's strengths instead of their weaknesses. Look for talent, and make sure it can be found."

So what is it like to dine in the dark? "People do behave differently than in a restaurant where the lights are on. They listen to each other more closely. They've got no choice, really, because talking and listening are the only possible forms of contact. Conversations in the dark tend to be more candid. People who don't know each other are more likely to strike up a conversation with people at nearby tables." Ctaste has meanwhile also started offering beer, wine, and cheese tasting sessions. "In the dark you can really put your taste buds to the test," says Ballij. "And it goes without saying that we are happy to cater to blind dates."

Profit motive

Literature about social enterprises makes ample mention of the concept of profit motive. A social enterprise's mission is, after all, primarily a social one, with financial objectives serving that mission. Does a social enterprise have to operate on a not-for-profit basis, or can it marry profit motive and its social mission, and if so, how much profit is it allowed to make and take? To us, it is ok for a social enterprise to turn a profit, and even to pay dividend, provided they strike a balance with both the mission and the best interests of all stakeholders. Investors and other financial backers are stakeholders too, and they deserve a reasonable return for their commitment, which is something quite different from ownership power and profit maximization. In practice, social entrepreneurs will tend to invest their profits in their companies to get closer to their social objective, in other words their reason for existence.

In the United Kingdom, this idea has been anchored in a legal entity that has been designed especially for social enterprises: the CIC, or Community Interest Company. By law, a CIC must invest at least 70 percent of its profits in the company, i.e. use it to achieve its statutorily intended social impact. The remaining 30 percent of profits can be paid out to shareholders.

Social enterprises are, in the words of José Durão Barroso, President of the European Commission, by definition social in their ends and means.* In other words: as a social enterprise, you want to fulfill your mission in a social way, be transparent, factor in the interests of all stakeholders,

* José Manuel Durão Barroso, President of the European Commission. *Building Responsible and Sustainable Growth — The Role of Social Entrepreneurs*, Social Innovation Conference, Brussels, 18 November 2011

and look after the environment. A true social entrepreneur walks the talk.

No enterprise without an entrepreneur. The entrepreneur is the man or woman who was moved to action and commits to the mission. In many ways, a social enterprise is far more difficult to set up than a regular enterprise, and setting up a regular enterprise is already something that few pull off. Running a social enterprise is a relentless pursuit: an unstoppable and tireless pursuit of making the mission a success, a personal and passionate pursuit, fired on by a drive that comes from deep within. This is where we find the beauty of the social entrepreneur that so inspires us. And that is what the next chapter is all about.

Specialisterren: autism at a perfectly ordinary company

They don't look like boys who can instantly recognize prime numbers and know the railroad timetable by heart. And you won't find Dustin Hoffman there either. It is basically a work-place like many other: about ten desks, computer screens, keyboards. Perhaps it's a bit tidier than most offices.

"No clean desk policy required," says Sjoerd van der Maaden, "they do that automatically, I don't have to tell them." He is one of the two founders and the managing director of Special-isterren, a software testing company. "The best testers" is the tagline in the logo under the company name. Is that so? Yes, it is, because Specialisterren's testers all have a form of autism. And autistic people just happen to have the gift of being able to concentrate better than "normal" people. Besides, they take things literally, making them extremely well suited for fairly monotonous work, which software testing inevitably is.

"This workplace here is untidy," we point out. Compared to the surrounding desks, it is, because in this orderly environment, you immediately notice an apple, tangerine peel, and a couple of pens lying unorganized next to a notepad. And the tester at this particular workplace, a headphones-wearing young man of about twenty years of age, is playing a video game on his second screen. "But he is very good. One of our star testers," says Sjoerd, a man in his fifties with a full head of curly hair and a pair of John Lennon-style glasses. "We won't disturb you any further, Bart." The young man lifts his headphone and says: "Thanks, I'm already disturbed enough."

Specialisterren was founded in 2010 by Van der Maaden and Ronald van Vliet, who had both worked in IT for years. "We ran into each other at interim jobs sometimes, and knew about each other's autistic children, which instantly created a bond. What will things be like when those boys, who are now only teenagers, grow up? They're smart boys, that's not it, but they're different. And they know they are, which often causes them to feel uncomfortable, as if they were social failures." Talking about their sons' future increasingly turned into a brainstorm about their own, about a company they could start together. "We've got to do it," they promised each other. As they looked for ways of making it happen, they came across Specialisterne, the Danish company founded by Thorkil Sonne. Two years later they had a solid business plan of their own.

"Why did it take that long?"

"We wanted to involve our stakeholders, our investors, potential customers and employees, and local authorities, and present our plan to them, and we adapted the plan to their wishes."

Specialisterren has particularly extensive dealings with the local authority — the city of Utrecht. "That's due to the fact that an autistic employee comes with a lot of institutional baggage: the employee insurance and welfare administration, a job coach, a case manager, a reintegration manager. It's like a procession." For the major part, the state wants the exact same as Van Der Maaden's company: to get people working.

Specialisterren saves the state a huge amount of money, as much as 848,000 euros in 2011. How do you get to that figure, the so-called social return on investment (SROI)? "We save the state money because the guys who work for us now only have one job coach, instead of twenty. And because three people who used to live in a residential support set-up are now living on their own. These are considerable savings: someone who does not work, costs the state about forty thousand euros a year. But we have also sought to attach financial value to the soft side. Take self-esteem, for example. My employees' self-esteem has shot up. Just imagine how much it would cost in terms of psychiatric sessions to raise someone's self-esteem. We have put that at fourteen hundred euros per person."

Relations with the local authority are good, they are well aware of how much value Specialisterren creates. "Better still, they are one of our customers: we test the software they use. They could do a lot more, if you ask me. By hiring, for example, people from us who have grown to such an extent that they can and want to work in a regular environment. Although where the state can be of most help to us is by improving access to funding, as getting a loan is really a major problem for us at present. Banks just don't want to take a risk on us, in a classic case of unknown, unloved. They see that although our figures are positive, our costs are higher and margins lower than those of our peers in the software testing industry. They would never say it out loud, but the way they see us is: 'Cute, a project with autistic boys, but they probably rely heavily on government subsidies.'"

This is a prejudice that Van Der Maaden faces often, but no, they receive zero subsidies. "We are a perfectly ordinary company, we have to offer value for money just like any other company. Sure, our customers like the idea of their software being tested by autistic IT professionals. Customers sometimes come to us for a performance evaluation. I handle these assessments together with one of our senior staff members, an autistic person. Customers find that fantastic, and that really makes me proud. Because the person at the table ceases to be an autistic person, and becomes a software testing professional. But at the end of the day, customers want value for money, they want quality, and that's exactly what they are getting." This also affects tester selection. "We receive open applications every week, but with a lot of these applicants I can see that they have tremendous capabilities, but know it just won't work. Because a job at our company does mean having to work 24 hours a week."

Van der Maaden and Van Vliet have made a considerable financial sacrifice. Both, one as a CFO and the other as a CTO, lived the IT boom around the turn of the century. The sky was the limit. Good times? "No, it was actually one of the reasons behind my decision to become a social entrepreneur. The IPO of the company I worked at made some of my nearest colleagues very rich indeed. Big cars in the parking lot. That's not really my thing I realized back then, that's not what drives me. I am extremely proud of the company we are building together, of the impact we're having. Still, there are also moments when Ronald and I ask ourselves what on earth we have gotten ourselves into. I always used to hold management positions, with responsibility for serious budgets. But I was never an entrepreneur, I never bore any risk, I was never going to get into trouble if we had a couple of bad months. But I am now: I have a family, three boys in college, and my youngest still lives at home. I'm not afraid to admit that things often get stressful."

How does Max feel about being a source of inspiration for his father's company?

"He likes it. I would really love to see him work at Specialisterren in the future. We'll have to wait a few years for that."

"Social entrepreneurs hail from all layers of society and form communities in virtually every single country in the world. They all have the same underlying drive and passion to make their ideas come true. Many have already had a massive impact on the world, although most people will not have heard of them — a situation we hope to change!"

Jeffrey Skoll, the first CEO of eBay and founder of Participant Media, Skoll Foundation and Skoll Centre for Social Entrepreneurship

2
Against the current

The special attributes of social entrepreneurs

What possesses someone to open a restaurant with visual- 37
ly impaired waiting staff? Who gets the idea to start an IT
company employing people with social interaction deficits
and who are regularly absent? A cab company with cars
that have to "refuel" after only 90 kilometers and can only
do so at three locations around Amsterdam? Launching a
fair supermarket chain and taking on the almighty Ahold?
Who does that, what kind of people are they, those social
entrepreneurs?

In most cases, social entrepreneurship requires a massive
all-round effort on top of the regular effort that goes into
being an entrepreneur: you need a firm theory of change,
be able to convert that into a sound business model, get
financial backers and other supporters on board, and
attract customers. Don't think social entrepreneurs are
greeted with applause wherever they go, often they are
met with skepticism, brushed aside as oddballs, not taken
seriously until they have proven the feasibility of their
enterprise. And on top of that, social entrepreneurs also
have to deal with the implicit or explicit view that you
should not make money from a social mission, as making
money is assumed to involve trampling on people and
is therefore intrinsically anti-social. Ctaste, for example,
was not welcomed with enthusiasm by the foundation for

the blind and the visually impaired, as they would much rather, in their role of protector of the blind and visually impaired, see their members not take a job and not jeopardize their welfare entitlements.

A social entrepreneur needs to be very sure of his or her mission and gather a group of like-minded people around him or her, otherwise it is very hard to see it through. In the words of Teun van de Keuken, founder of Tony's Chocolonely: "Working on this for so long and speaking to so many former slaves has instilled great commitment in me. I hope to be able to open people's eyes to abuses in the cocoa industry. I don't know what an ideal world looks like and it's not something I believe in, but it's important that people think about certain things." Teun found that, as a journalist, just writing about it wasn't enough, that he would only be making a real difference when slavery-free chocolate is readily available from supermarkets, giving consumers a socially responsible option. And he took that as his mission, because otherwise it would never happen.

Teun's story is a very special one, but at the same time also a very normal one among the stories of social entrepreneurs.

Sandra Ballij of Ctaste gave up her career, her salary, her company car at ING Bank to open a restaurant with blind waiting staff. When she first experienced the concept, she said to herself, jokingly: that looks like fun, let's open a place like that in Amsterdam. But it soon became inescapable — she really had to do it, she felt compelled. Although she lacked any kind of experience in the restaurant business, she had real passion to make a difference, to empower people. It was very tangible, very big.

Ruud Zandvliet and Edvard Hendriksen, both 29, friends from college, were making very nice careers for them-

selves in the telecommunications and financial world. But
then they started thinking: "We are all just wrecking the
place, we're en route to an ecological and social disaster.
People living in Amsterdam die a few years sooner than
those living elsewhere in the Netherlands due to poor
air quality, and we simply sideline large groups of very
competent people. That's just not right. We want to show
that there's another way." Taxi Electric was born.

And Sjoerd van der Maaden of Specialisterren? As a
frontrunner of working with autistic people in the Netherlands, he makes only a fraction of his previous comfortable
typical IT industry salary, but he is asked to speak at conferences every week to share his story to inspire others.

This book compiles many of these exceptional stories,
which to social entrepreneurs themselves, are very normal
stories.

A stubborn lunatic

In October 2012, the first ever meeting of Social Enterprise NL, the Netherlands society for social enterprises,
was attended by around forty social entrepreneurs. Upon
receiving his invitation to this event, Henry Mentink of
MyWheels said, with some level of surprise: "So MyWheels
is a social enterprise?" Indeed it is, Henry, and you are a
social entrepreneur. For many years, he had been doing
what social entrepreneurs do, but was never labeled a
social entrepreneur. It was about time. There was a high
degree of unanimity in the feedback at the meeting, aptly
summarized by the words of Ties Kroezen of NICE International, who quit his management consultancy job to
go and live in Senegal with his family and return to the
Netherlands a social entrepreneur: "It's very encouraging
to find out that I'm not the only stubborn lunatic who is
trying to do something like this in the Netherlands."

Fairphone: "open" on all counts

Bas van Abel, founder of Fairphone, launched a campaign three years ago to raise awareness of abuses in the production of electronic devices. He chose the smartphone as an example. One smartphone contains over thirty kinds of metal, including copper, cobalt, tin, gold, and nickel. These raw materials primarily come from the Democratic Republic of the Congo. In the Katanga province alone, an estimated 150,000 people work in mines, including over 50,000 adolescents and children.

Bas decided to design his own phone. He sourced the materials for his Fairphone from "fair" mines and tried to recycle materials as much as possible. He succeeded step by step. For the production of his phone, Van Abel chose a former state-owned company in China which previously produced for the Chinese internal market only: "A smaller factory allows you to experiment and grow together." Fairphone will set up a fund at the factory that both parties will pay into. Money from that fund must be used for further training and improvement of working conditions for all employees.

Where other manufacturers impose their corporate identity and prohibit users from disassembling their phones, Fairphones will come with an open-source Android operating system, and make it easy to replace parts yourself. "We believe the Fairphone is to be a phone that is "open" on all counts," says Van Abel.

Openness is what Fairphone is all about. The company creates dialog between all parties, from policymaker to consumer, from designer to marketer. Van Abel: "Electronics is now in the same situation as the clothing industry was about twenty years ago. If we all refuse to accept the current situation, things can change rapidly. Because we are actually making this phone, we are showing that there is a different way." That users appreciate that became clear when 10,000 devices were pre-ordered through crowdfunding.

Marqt's Quirijn Bolle put it as follows: "In the early days, people sometimes don't even give you the time of day. You really need to be sure of yourself. At times I felt like a tight-rope walker: if you get to the other side, you're a visionary, but if you fall off along the way, you're the village idiot. There's no in between."

An international study of social entrepreneurs, published in the highly readable book *The Power of Unreasonable People* (2008) by John Elkington and Pamela Hartigan, provides an accurate description of the character of a social entrepreneur. A small and recognizable selection from the character traits:

- focus first and foremost on creating social value and is, in that same vein, willing to share his or her innovations and insights for others to replicate
- show a dogged determination that pushes them to take risks others wouldn't dare
- have an unwavering belief in everyone's innate capacity, often regardless of education, to contribute meaningfully to economic and social development
- jump in before assuring they are fully resourced.

A particularly interesting trait is the *willingness to share innovations and insights*, because while commercial entrepreneurs consider others competitors, social entrepreneurs see others as colleagues. That's very logical in their situation. If what you want to do is rid the world of slavery, you welcome any initiative by someone else that seeks to do the same. Social entrepreneurs have a strong sense of peer solidarity.

Dogged determination and an *unwaveringbelief* alone are not enough for success. Starting a regular business is already something few manage to do successfully, let alone a social enterprise. A few years back, *The Journal*

of Business Ethics published* an extensive study through
which the researchers hoped to discover which traits boost
social entrepreneurs' chance of success, with a view to
increasing business courses' focus on developing these
traits. What did the study show? Social entrepreneurs
are good-natured, meticulous, open, innovative, perfor-
mance-driven, independent, do not shy away from risk,
and tolerate ambiguity. The conclusion: social entrepreneurship requires a combination of mind and heart, of
knowledge and virtue.

Social entrepreneurs are willing to swim against the
current, mainly because theirs are often products and
services that haven't yet proven themselves, generally
made in a way that hasn't been used before, using models
that have not yet been accepted as a solution to problems
that not everyone considers to be problems yet. More than
ten years ago, Yunus had to fight for his Grameen Bank
to be taken seriously, and it took another ten years for his
bank to break even. Microfinance has meanwhile become
mainstream. Or take climate change, a social problem
that many still find nonsense, a fabrication. Long before
even the most ardent skeptics recognize a problem, the
solution will require investment and work. You can only
overcome those tough years with a lot of drive and passion,
by striking up partnerships with inspiring stakeholders on
every level, from employees to investors, and by wanting
to change something in society and beyond through that
monomaniacal mission.

In balance
Financial health is essential, both for enterprise and entrepreneur. Recent research published in *Harvard Business*

* *Journal of Business Ethics* (2010) 95, p. 260

*Review** showed that social entrepreneurs who have coupled their social mission with a profit motive are more successful than those who focus solely on social impact. Financial health means your company has something saved up for a rainy day and is able to absorb bad periods of lower turnover, without that causing critical problems. And, in any case, it means being able to pay yourself a decent wage, which is very important. Compare it to the safety instructions on a plane: in case of an emergency, the oxygen masks will drop out of the ceiling. "Put your own oxygen mask on first," the instruction says, "and then help your children." You can only help someone else when you yourself are well. That is the challenge many inspired entrepreneurs face.

The entrepreneur is faced with dilemmas in striking the right balance between financial health and social impact. These two objectives have a tendency to clash. What is an entrepreneur supposed to do when things aren't going well? Lay people off, even though the mission is to get people working again? Will he or she turn to conventional production methods after all, perhaps not completely organic or carbon neutral? But also when things are plain sailing, dilemmas arise: what should a social entrepreneur do with a surplus? How should he or she invest profits? A social entrepreneur who is doing well and growing his or her business is often contacted by parties — such as investors — who want to buy in. What are their motives? Mission drift is lurking, how strong are you and what choices will you make? Will you go for growth? Or will you pave the way for others to copy your model to achieve even greater impact? These are common dilemmas for social entrepreneurs.

* Research by the Endeavor Sealing Social Impact Insight Center, published online by *Harvard Business Review*, hbr.org, 9 January 2013

Thuisafgehaald: sharing food with the neighbors

Do you like to cook? Also for others? And do you think they will like your food? Or don't you cook, but would you still like to have a nice meal at home? Either way, Thuisafgehaald (Home take-out) is there for you, as it provides a platform where home chefs and take-out enthusiasts can find each other. Marieke Hart got the idea for this website when she smelled her neighbor's soup and cheekily went over to ask for a bowl. Besides a bowl of soup, she also got closer contact with that neighbor. It eventually inspired the concept for www.thuisafgehaald.nl, where amateur cooks offer a home-made meal to local residents for a few euros.

This initiative serves multiple purposes. One important goal is to reduce food wastage. "Every year, we throw away about 50 kilos of food per person. At Thuisafgehaald, a take-out customer gets a measured portion. And whenever someone has cooked too much food one day, they can simply offer it for sale the next day." Besides that, the social effect often goes beyond merely making an appointment and picking up the food. "What we are seeing is that people who buy meals from the same cook on various occasions also end up having contacts that do not involve a food purchase. That can be taking care of the cat, or lending each other a book, for example."

Within a year, Thuisafgehaald had 40,000 members, and it is adding around 150 every day. Meanwhile, around 200 meals are shared every day, while the total tally already stands at 100,000. "A huge success, although it is currently still mainly concentrated in cities." Thuisafgehaald has already received a bucket load of publicity and won an innovation award from Accenture.

3

More than just money

*The unusual business model of social
enterprises*

Imagine that huge factory near your home were to burst
into flames. Hopefully it won't happen, of course, but it's
possible. What will happen? The fire brigade would turn
out and extinguish the fire. The insurance company would
send experts and assess the damage. Another company
would clear up the mess. A bit further down the line, an
architect is commissioned to design a new building, after
which the contractor can start constructing it. Six months
later, new machines are delivered and the general manager opens his new factory with a big smile on his face. The
fire has effectively triggered a chain of activities, each
and every one of which are benefiting the economy, our
country's gross domestic product. So the fire was good for
the economy, provided you interpret the economy as the
financial economy, in the way that the Secretary of the
Treasury does.

But is that not odd? The factory was in good shape before
it went up in flames, the machines did not need replacing
just yet. And although attempts were made to clean up
the fallout from the fire, contaminated fire extinguishing
water still ended up in the soil and the smoke, which was
probably not very clean, was released into the air. The same
goes for plane crashes, smoking, and wars: they are widely
claimed to be good for the economy. So what's good for the
financial economy is not by definition good for people.

Social entrepreneurs focus on social value, on what's good for people, and are not blinded by dollar signs. Having your next-door neighbor mind your child instead of taking your child to daycare is not good for the financial economy, but may be good for your child, for you, and for your next-door neighbor. A social entrepreneur is not after maximization of financial gains. To a social entrepreneur, money is a means to an end, not an end in its own right, and when you stop and think about that, you wonder how

it can be any other way really. Have we perhaps lost our way at some point? Shrouds have no pockets, and money cannot buy happiness. Money is a means of exchange, no more. What it should be about is, in our view, to create value for society — and society, that's us. Profits for everyone, and not profits for some at the expense of others.

Value added

Many social enterprises seem very ordinary businesses, such as a restaurant, a cab company, or a chocolate maker. But they are run by entrepreneurs who are pursuing socialization of existing markets, from the foundations up; they are showing there's another way. And that is where ethical and ecological frontrunners, such as Triodos Bank and Tony's Chocolonely add value. Ctaste's website does not give you any insight into the value this enterprise has for blind people. You pay for a fun experience, the entrepreneur makes a reasonable living, and staff get paid. And that's where the value is added, because that salary gives blind people independence, changing their role from care recipient to someone who is important to the team, and greatly boosting their self-esteem. This is not a certainty...

An entrepreneur takes on a tremendous challenge when he or she sets out to make his or her enterprise add value in this way. It requires very special competency as a leader and as a company. Specialisterren, for example, has an important competency that is situated between care and management. How do you make people with autism productive and customer-oriented? Taxi Electric has to manage with electric vehicles with a limited range, but they do get something in return. It is that focus on the positive that gives strength.

Social enterprises will need to look for innovative solutions to incorporate the value they seek to add, and the additional costs that entails, in a healthy business plan. And also for other ways of interacting, for different relationships with partners and customers. Take the concept of Pay What You Want, for example: providing a service first and only then "engaging" the customer on what he or she is willing to pay. It has turned out to work perfectly at dozens of restaurants across the United States. Many entrepreneurs are showing that it can be done, that consumers have an open mind and are accessible, also when it comes to social value, such as at Triodos or Tony's.

But there are also entrepreneurs who take things one step further, who are looking for entirely new business models, for other forms of value creation. These pioneers face an even more difficult task, as they will struggle even more to prove themselves financially. Both groups are important, because no matter how revolutionary and innovative the pioneers are, the movement of social entrepreneurs would be (and will always remain) a small one if none would accept the existing models. Last year, one Dutch academic, Professor Jan Jonker, conducted a study*

* Jan Jonker in collaboration with Marloes Tap and Tim van Straaten, Working Paper 'Duurzaam Organiseren' [Sustainable Organization], Nijmegen School of Management — Radboud Universiteit Nijmegen, 1 June 2012

Zorgvoorelkaar *(Careforeachother)*: e-dating for self-reliance

Picture an 86-year-old lady. Her dearest wish is to visit the grave of her deceased daughter in Leiden. She lives in Etten-Leur and has no family who can take her and her wheelchair to Leiden by car. Her wish is converted into a task and posted on the online marketplace called Zorgvoorelkaar (Taking care of each other). Two weeks later, a young woman who responded to the advert drives the old lady to Leiden. That's taking care of each other. And this is very badly needed, according to Patrick Anthonissen and Mathijs Huis in 't Veld, who launched Zorgvoorelkaar in early 2012: an online platform where people with care or assistance needs are linked to volunteers or professionals. It's like e-dating for care and assistance.

"We really have to start taking care of each other a lot more. Because those cuts in the residential care budget totaling nearly one billion euros will have to be compensated for by volunteers. An expected 220,000 additional volunteers are needed. And we at Zorgvoorelkaar want to make taking care of each other easy and fun, and lower the threshold."

Where local authorities and care providers often fail, Zorgvoorelkaar succeeds: the platform has managed to engage a young target group. The average age of the 1,300 volunteers registered on Zorgvoorelkaar is forty, while 20 percent of volunteers is aged below twenty-five.

Local authorities like doing business with Zorgvoorelkaar: the Social Support Act bestows responsibility for care for the elderly and disabled people on local authorities, but they often lack resources. They benefit greatly from this kind of online marketplace that unlocks resources that help increase self-reliance and civic engagement. Zorgvoorelkaar's revenue model is therefore based on contract agreements with local authorities and care organizations.

into new business models that create multiple value, and found two important new — or rather very old — models: sharing and exchanging.

Sharing

Clear examples of social enterprises that revolve around sharing in the Netherlands are Snappcar and MyWheels, which go a lot further than mere car sharing. The cars you can find through their websites are almost all privately owned vehicles that you can rent. The underlying idea of both these initiatives is obvious: there are too many cars and most are barely used. You want figures? There are currently 7 million cars in the Netherlands, and that number is set to rise to 9 million, which makes one car for every two inhabitants. On average, a car is used to drive 30 kilometers a day, and unused 23 hours a day. 1 million cars could therefore be more than enough for the Netherlands. Just imagine, it would be paradise! No traffic jams, no parking problems, no more car-lined streets. And less car production would, of course, also save raw materials. Another important objective of these initiatives is to forge social cohesion: you get to know your neighbors, as you share each other's property.

Downsizing the Netherlands' fleet of vehicles to one million is not very likely, because so many people are very attached to their wheels. But this susceptibility to status symbols is not something everyone has, and does not apply to all products.

Car sharing is an attractive and well-known example and we are seeing other forms of this trend emerging now. Peerby, for example, is a young online platform that enables private individuals to borrow and rent all kinds of things from people in their community. Peerby has set out to get people into contact with people in their community they do not know. This way, the platform makes an enter-prising and surprising contribution to social cohesion in a neighborhood. As neighbors borrow things from each other, they get to know each other, which helps inspire solidarity and a sense of security. Apart from that, Peerby also helps reduce waste and cut energy consumption. Another fine example is Thuisafgehaald (see page 44), one of the Netherlands' fastest-growing sharing platforms. Sharing is not limited to physical products, it also applies to services, to doing something for each other, as shown by Zorgvoorelkaar (see page 48).

This movement is showing a considerable surge, not only inspired by noble motives such as environmental awareness and the realization that we are overproducing and overconsuming, but also propelled by the influence of government taxes and incentives. Various raw materials are becoming scarcer and more expensive, so expensive in fact that it has become financially attractive for manufac-turers to keep and recycle them.

Part of the essence of sharing is the social aspect. In a program on Dutch TV,* American writer Douglas Rush-koff used the following anecdote to illustrate this aspect: "My family lived in a fairly poor neighborhood in New York City. The park around the corner had a barbecue that anyone from the neighborhood could use. Every Sunday, the whole neighborhood converged on the park and cooked food there. One person brought hot dogs, another a steak, and you would all eat together. Then my dad got another job and we moved to a better neighbor-hood. There was no communal barbecue at the bottom of the street there, but everyone had their own barbecue. What happened? On Sundays, everyone would stay in

* *Tegenlicht*, VPRO, 28 January 2013

their own garden, not barbecuing with but against the neighbors, everyone was trying to outdo each other on price and quality of the meat they would throw on their grill."

Bartering

Barter is even older than the hills: it was the dominant economic model before money made its appearance. In the 1930s, barter made a return, initially only in Canada, when the economic crisis of the time caused entire village populations to lose their jobs, making barter the only way to get food and work. Barter has developed since then, moved beyond the old one-on-one requirement: one loaf of bread for a pound of apples, a bag of rice in exchange for a dental procedure. Barter systems now often go by the name of LETS, or Local Exchange Trading System, which often have their own currency. One well-known example is the Brixton Pound, an accepted means of payment in the London district of Brixton, intended to stimulate the local economy, while also strengthening social cohesion. The faces of celebrities with Brixton roots, such as David Bowie, adorn Brixton pound notes, and the system has recently also gone electronic, enabling Brixton pound payments by text message. These systems grow into new and complementary money flows and are social enterprises in their own right, bringing prosperity and cohesion to a community.

There are numerous LETS all over the world, and their number is growing rapidly. That is no surprise: as in the 1930s, an economic crisis has swept across large parts of the world, making LETS the only way some people can create value and keep an economy going. A major difference in comparison to the 1930s is the use of IT: it is extremely easy for people to find each other on online

Noppes: rich together

Forget dollars, euros, and pounds: nops are what you need! A black karate uniform, size L, cotton, comfy to wear: 20 nops. An organic apple pie: 8 nops. Founded in 1993, Noppes is the Netherlands' oldest local exchange trading system (LETS). Its over 600 members, most of whom are based in Amsterdam, offer things for sale on a website, ranging from second-hand items to services such as babysitting, copywriting, and IT help. Alternative lifestyle antics by silly hippies? Not at all, Noppes also has doctors and lawyers among its members. Noppes serves a social and an economic purpose. On the one hand, people (probably those doctors) take the exchange trading system as amusing and creative, and as a fun way of helping someone out, while on the other hand, it broadens people's — such as someone who's unemployed — spending power.

The value of a nop equals one euro, but nops are never exchanged for euros. The annual membership fee, however, is paid in euros (and nops), as are possible direct expenses incurred for your service. Members are advised to offer their service for a fee of between 5 and 15 nops an hour, which are rather low rates when you consider the euro value. Your nop balance is registered like a bank would do, and just like some bank accounts, you can also be in the red, up to a maximum of 100 nops (without the excessive interest and threatening reminders). "Nops must roll, they're not intended for savings. When you have sold something, the idea is that you spend the nops you made," says the website.

"It's not about the dough, but about the idea of being rich together," one participant explains. "We are in no way against the euro. This is a complementary system. The main thing is the idea that you can also do fun and useful things without money." One of the goals is therefore to move participants from dependency to reciprocity: you can always contribute, and not only when you have a job. Members who are on welfare are not required to report their Noppes earnings to the Department for Work and Income (DWI). "You can trade to your heart's content," the website states, "as long as you abide by arrangements with the DWI and remain available for the job market." And although these wheelings and dealings take place outside the financial economy, the tax man still keeps an eye on it: as soon as someone's earnings top 3,000 nops in a year, he or she is liable to pay tax on their earnings.

Noppes is run by volunteers and has not yet grown into a complementary currency system. Similar initiatives elsewhere have indeed reached that status, such as the Brixton Pound.

Want to join one too? Check www.letscontact.nl for a local exchange trading system near you!

networks, and supply and demand are often matched very quickly. Besides, nowadays these networks run on software that is very affordable or even free altogether thanks to open source and freeware. A variation on a LETS is the so-called time bank, where you pay in time dollars, meaning that you use your time as a means of payment. And seeing as a lawyer's minute is just as long as a cleaner's minute, time banks work in a highly egalitarian fashion.

Basically, these new complementary currency systems take us back to where we were when money was first introduced: a closed group of people who trust each other and want to do business with each other based on these "points systems."

We can conclude that the models social enterprises use to achieve their impact are highly diverse. Some are based on the current economy and make existing models social, while others attempt to set up a completely different and new economy, based on principles such as barter and sharing.

A different relation to each other is, of course, not obvious. How do you do that? Customers must want it and be willing to pay for it, but how much? At the end of the day, they want value for money. And who exactly are those customers?

Fifteen: meant to be

It's called Fifteen, and not because it is based at number 15 or because the menu of the day always costs 15 euros. The name comes from the fact that this restaurant trains fifteen maladjusted youths to work in the hospitality industry every year. Celebrity chef Jamie Oliver started it in London, and Sarriel Taus is the man behind the Amsterdam branch. "I read about it and instantly knew: I want to do this in the Netherlands," Taus says. Experience in the restaurant business? No. Entrepreneurial spirit and passion? Yes! After two years and numerous meetings with regional training centers, reintegration agencies, local authorities, and Jamie himself, he finally opened his Fifteen in 2004.

The restaurant is located on the Amsterdam harborfront. It's an old warehouse, very sleek, hip, with graffiti art on the walls. The kitchen is open plan, so diners can see the chef rule the roost and his apprentices man the pans, wearing their white hats. "At the start of the year, they are barely able to fry an egg." But after one year, they have a vocational qualification and invaluable experience at Fifteen that will land them a job almost anywhere. "And we are not making things easy for ourselves: we're not in the business of picking low-hanging fruit. For most of the boys and girls we take in, Fifteen was truly their last chance. In speeches I often say jokingly: 'We won't let you in if you don't have prison time on your résumé.'" Do things ever go wrong? "Yes, sure, there was one instance where one apprentice chased another around the kitchen wielding a ten-liter pan of Bolognese sauce, which ended up all over our guests. But our chef is not the Gordon Ramsay type, because a bully like that would cause major problems in our kitchen, these boys need love, and clarity."

Fifteen has now been going for nearly ten years, and is a household name in the Netherlands. That is no mean feat: many businesses in the hospitality industry don't survive that long, let alone restaurants with the self-imposed handicap of maladjusted staff. What is the reason behind its success? The restaurant partly owes its success to the high profile Jamie Oliver brings to the place, as well as to an eight-part reality series about the Amsterdam branch that aired on Dutch TV in 2004: Fifteen has always had its PR and marketing in order, it presents itself very well. "But," Taus adds, "it is first and foremost down to the quality of the food we serve. Although our apprentices may be inexperienced, their chef is top class. And that's the bottom line, because people don't come to eat here because our staff members are disadvantaged," says Taus, himself a clumsy amateur cook, but also the CTO: *Chief Tasting Officer*. And, of course, also thanks to the training allowance Fifteen receives from the employee insurance and welfare administration. Would Fifteen survive without the government welfare support for the youngsters? "Of course, we would also be able to be a good restaurant and training center without public funds," says Taus, "but we would then have to charge 60 euros per meal, which would be too far above normal market prices."

Their cupboard is always bare, metaphorically speaking, because even with government funding things are difficult financially. "Remember: my chef is not paid for the additional work of preparing these youngsters for the job market. He is on the payroll for a forty-hour working week. But I've added twenty hours to that, for coaching duties, to train our apprentices. Unpaid. When you work at Fifteen, you know that comes with the job. That's your contribution to society." Laughingly: "But you also get karma points!"

Fortunately, Taus is a very competent networker, with a keen business mind and very creative. You could perhaps even say that he has entrepreneurial skills to spare — and for that reason alone, Fifteen is surviving. "I am a social entrepreneur, with the emphasis on entrepreneur. That means being able to adapt to changing circumstances. Is the government about to cut funding for reintegration projects? Make sure you have a plan B. And C and D. This is often what's lacking at other organizations with a social mission: as soon as funding is cut, they get stuck. If government funding were to be cut completely, Fifteen would not survive. This is where the Amsterdam branch differs from Fifteen HQ in the UK: there are greater problems with youths there, but at the same time there is also greater commitment from the population. Whenever Jamie Oliver organizes a charity dinner, he can count on Richard Branson to happily pay top dollar. We've tried it here as well, but we struggled to sell tables, and only sold ten in the end. The Dutch mentality is one of "we pay taxes, let the government deal with it."

"You know," Taus continues, "I can't quite put my finger on it yet, but it bothers me somehow. As a social entrepreneur, you create value for the whole world, and that value is not always captured in traditional value that will, for example, be reason for a bank to grant you a loan. Here's how it works: Fifteen provides young people with good training before they enter the job market, saving the state perhaps as many as thirty years of welfare payments. And that in an industry that is only seeing its customer base shrink as the Dutch population ages."

"Was it hard work?" we ask at the end of our conversation, expecting the standard entrepreneurs' answer, something along the lines of: "Yeah, eight days a week." Taus: "No, not really. I always try to use gravity in everything I do. When you find you have to push hard to get something done, it is probably not to be. But when things are meant to be, a tiny push is often all it takes to set things rolling. That was the case with Fifteen."

Taus left Fifteen in November 2013. "Ten years was a nice round number. It was time to go. Better for me, better for Fifteen. Although I still had a lot of plans for Fifteen, at some point you just realize the party's over." And now? "I have no idea yet as to what I'm going to do. I initially thought about going into the cultural sector, thinking my being a business whiz with his heart in the right place would mean I could make a difference there, but my headhunter soon pointed out that I am far too unconventional for that. I am now doing something very exciting though, something about making the world's tastiest hamburger. And I also have more time for another project of mine, the *Zuidermarkt*, a market for organic foods in my neighborhood in the southern part of Amsterdam. And I'm going to write a book about running a business with friends, which is something that mostly ends in broken friendships, and I ask: why is that, what's the secret?"

"I'm extremely proud of what I've built," Taus says. "Fifteen is an icon. Spin-offs have popped up all over the place. The other day I read an article in the paper about a restaurant that opened in Breda and somehow has a social mission, and the standard comparison they made was to call it 'a kind of Fifteen.' And you know, we made it happen without the big name, Jamie. We have trained 150 youths since we opened. What never ceases to fill me with great pride is when I'm eating somewhere and find out that the sous chef is one of our boys. But it doesn't matter where you work, whether it be a Michelin-starred restaurant or a burger joint, as long as you have taken charge of your life and made something of yourself, that's what's most important." Just a drop in the ocean? "That's not how I think. It always makes me think of that story about a girl who goes for a walk on a beach that is littered with thousands of dying jellyfish. She picks one up and carefully returns it to the sea. A passer-by asks: 'What good does that do?' The girl replies: 'A lot for that one jellyfish.'"

4

Companies with a story

Positioning a social enterprise

You buy something, probably every day. You consume,
you pay for services. Perhaps not only in your private life,
but also on behalf of the organization where you work. As
a consumer, you choose one and not the other, you vote
with your feet, you decide with your wallet. And day after
day, stores, manufacturers, or suppliers try their best to get
you to spend your money with them. As do social enterprises. Because social enterprises, too, can only exist when
they manage to win over customers, get them to select
their product or service and pay a price that at least lets
the social enterprise break even. How do social enterprises
stay afloat amid these commercial forces?

A social enterprise simply needs to offer a good product or service at a reasonable price. But that is certainly not as straightforward as it sounds, because a social
enterprise often accepts a competitive disadvantage.
Ensuring the cocoa chain is slavery-free makes the chain
more complex, and consequently the end product more
expensive for the customer than those of less responsible
competitors. A blind waiter cannot serve as quickly as a
seeing one, and an autistic person may be an awesomely
meticulous tester, working a full week at speed is beyond
them and they will be absent now and again. Needless to
say, this makes it hard to run a tight ship.

The entrepreneur has his or her goal, his or her mission,

but the "why" is not the product. Henk Jan Beltman, Chief Chocolate Officer at Tony's Chocolonely puts it as follows: "We're about slavery-free, not about chocolate. It might just as well have been another product. As soon as major companies go slavery-free, we will probably tackle the next chain, such as coffee." Specialisterren wants to help autistic people get a job and their customers want their software tested properly. That is clear and exactly what Specialisterren does. But what does the mission mean to the customer, and what can the social enterprise do with that knowledge? Is the mission an advantage that can be used to somewhat compensate for the abovementioned competitive disadvantage? Will customers be willing to pay a premium for it or accept a different attitude or service?

Storytelling

A number of social enterprises explicitly target their marketing efforts on conscious consumers, roughly 8 percent of the population, who are referred to as *cultural creatives*. This group is made up of consumers who have more spending power than the average Dutchman, and besides quality and price also consider the story behind the product. Tony's Chocolonely and Fifteen very explicitly target these consumers. The underlying mission helps position the brand.

Toms, a hip and social American shoe and eyewear brand that tries to attract customers with the slogan "Buy One, Give One," has incorporated its cause into its concept: for every pair of shoes or glasses sold, the company will donate one to a child in a poor country. Its founder, Blake Mycoskie, realized that his company's growth was spurred by the fact that customers passed on the story behind Toms. Customers who diffuse the brand story become brand ambassadors. This will only happen if yours is a story that is worth supporting and that people want to be a part of. And if you have partners who want more than to just buy and sell fashionable shoes and eyewear, but are also interested in supporting the social mission.

ONEforONE has become a marketing concept that appeals to conscious consumers. This does not mean, however, that cause-related marketing alone makes a company a social enterprise, because that classification is earned based on a broader set of characteristics. A social enterprise is, you could say, the union of a company and a social cause, and has the ability to let its social objective speak for itself. It will have to try to turn the disadvantage of a dual or triple bottom line into an advantage. They have to find a very subtle way of doing that, because an overbearing mission can detract from the product. Ultimately, what matters most is the customer experience, in other words the service or the product.

Fifteen and Tony's have both opted for a very modern and cool concept. That's the basis. Yumeko, an online eco-friendly linen and towel store, is another example. Their approach is illustrated by a recent advertising campaign, with adverts that read: "*Slaap zzzacht*" (Sleep sssoftly), and the following punchline below that: "*De wereld is al hard genoeg*" (The world is hard enough as it is). So first the product, and then the underlying mission. That is what we are seeing: successful social enterprises not immediately pushing their social credentials into the limelight. They leave that to the second instance, on the packaging, the website (perhaps not even on the homepage), or through staff.

Consumers buy into the mission, because the mission is the value added, provided it is presented in an appealing manner, which marketing professionals refer to as "storytelling." These stories need to be genuine stories about the

Return to Sender: trade with a good story

Bags, jewelry, scarves, but since recently also chocolate from Senegal, Sri Lanka, Cambodia and other poor countries: this is just a random selection of products that Dutch retail chain HEMA sells under the Return to Sender label. Return to Sender is a special partnership between a social project and a department store, which came about when the woman behind the project, Dutch actress Katja Schuurman, ran into HEMA managing director Ronald van Zetten on the set of a Dutch TV talk show in 2007.

Schuurman had just launched Return to Sender: her intention was to combat poverty by selling traditionally manufactured products from some of the world's poorest regions in the rich West. "Many people think: poverty is such a huge problem, what can I do about it? Let someone else solve it. But consumers have a great deal of power. Consumers can impact on companies' policy by choosing or not choosing to buy things. Fair trade products therefore need to be attractive and fun."

The HEMA retail chain turned out to be an ideal partner when they offered to carry Return to Sender products. HEMA not only cleared shelf space, but also provided guidance on design and other marketing aspects to make sure local producers actually make things that will sell. Schuurman: "The orders we place are an economic impulse for the regions where the products come from, and we can use our profits to start new projects."

For HEMA, the Return to Sender partnership fits into their existing corporate social responsibility programs. HEMA has been donating old workwear for years, destining funds raised through the tips jar to various charities, and takes a responsible approach to energy consumption and waste at all their stores. The company's goal of "making people's lives nicer and easier" comes to the fore in the Return to Sender line, which in terms of its appearance is consistent with the HEMA corporate identity and makes it easier for customers to make a valuable contribution to combating poverty.

A fine partnership that benefits many parties: local producers, who are the beneficiaries of Return to Sender's projects, the HEMA retail chain that can use the collaboration to raise its corporate citizenship profile, the customers who are buying attractive products with a good story, and the foundation itself, which currently employs twelve people.

product, preferably coming directly from the people who make it. Stories that are engaging, that consumers "want to be a part of," that consumers want to tell others about, and that in the best-case scenario have the power to turn a consumer into a brand ambassador. Credible and personal are keywords in this context, as well as a prerequisite for engagement.

What do you want to show?
At the Fifteen restaurant, customers can see the youngsters at work, while waiters at Ctaste are blind. Does that help? A bar of tasty chocolate with a backstory is one thing, but what happens when customers are also directly confronted with the mission and expected to actively commit to it? That is asking a lot of customers, and some social entrepreneurs find it hard to stomach when that turns out to be asking too much.

That is the tough lesson Paul Malschaert of the *Opdrachtenbank*, a web communication company that employs people with a physical disability learned. The reason why his company missed out on orders at the very last moment on several occasions, while they offered at least equal quality, slowly became clear: clients were impressed with the company's noble social intentions and were pleased to shortlist the *Opdrachtenbank* in the bidding procedure. But when push came to shove, doubts crept in, because the *Opdrachtenbank* is, at the end of the day, different. Imagine you contract that social crew and things don't turn out so well, you as procurement officer will get a lot of stick from your boss. Paul decided to try to make the best of it, adjusted his marketing approach and removed the wheelchairs from the website. His company is now called Swink web services. The mission is clearly described on the website, albeit not on the homepage.

Specialisterren has found that its employees' autism does have a sales-boosting effect: visiting clients are taken with the staff and have a nice story to tell at home. But Specialisterren has a powerful story behind it, based on the fact that their impairment makes autistic people 30 percent better at this work than others. And yet clients have to overcome a barrier, if only because autistic people really communicate differently. They're not very good at breaking bad news gently — they just come out with it, saying what's good and what's not. That is not common practice, not even in IT, so customers must be willing to get used to that. Specialisterren and Swink will have to find customers who are willing and dare to take this step, knowing that they will get a very special service in return.

What customers want first and foremost is quality at a good price, with a special experience thrown in. Naturally, there are people for whom a product's social mission is the primary reason for buying it, and who are willing to settle for lower quality or pay a substantial premium, which they can apparently afford, but that group is small. And because that group is small, the product will not be scalable, and consequently not have the impact the entrepreneur has in mind. A social enterprise needs to be very aware of its strengths, and of what problem they face when the "why" and the "what" are different things. The why is an additional experience or engaging factor, but to the majority of customers it is not more than that.

That is also how things work at the *Nationale Postcode Loterij*: many participants start playing in the hope of winning prizes (and out of a fear of the neighbor winning and them missing out), but they keep playing because of the satisfaction supporting charities awards them. In marketing terms: make your social commitment your main differentiating power.

Needless to say, we cannot pinpoint which marketing approach will work for a social entrepreneur due to the great diversity in social enterprises. After all, Tony's Chocolonely differs enormously from a software firm. But still, we feel that every starting social entrepreneur should take a time-out as soon as he or she has established a social mission and the accompanying product or service is in place. Put your plan to one side, and have a think about your marketing. How are you going to position your brand? Who are your customers? How are you going to approach them? How will you seize a relevant market share, and what about scalability? And if you are unable to thrash out a marketing plan, you must make sure you get someone on your team who can.

Merchant or minister?

Social entrepreneurs can also suffer the bad luck of having a social mission that doesn't really appeal to people or tackles an issue that consumers don't yet see as an issue and therefore is too far ahead of its time. Charities can tell you a thing or two about that: caring for wounded

Max Havelaar: a household name

Launched in 1988 as a quality label for coffee sourced from farmers or plantations that receive a fair price for their product, the label is now also used on bananas, wine, tea, spices, ice cream, peanut butter, and even on cotton products and flowers: walk into any local supermarket in the Netherlands, and you cannot miss the green-black-and-blue logo.

This Dutch initiative has been exported to as many as twenty-three countries, although not under the Max Havelaar name, but instead under a new name, Fairtrade International. The logo was retained and the umbrella organization was named FLO (Fairtrade Labelling Organizations International). The Max Havelaar Foundation is not a social enterprise, but it still deserves a mention in this book on account of its huge impact on consumer behavior. Or better still, on the lives of a great number of farmers in developing countries, currently euphemistically referred to as the bottom of the pyramid: people who live on less than 1 dollar a day.

Max Havelaar has shown that Western consumers are indeed susceptible to the social component of their spending pattern. Marketing coffee without running market research first, with the intention of making life better for the farmers who produce the beans: that is, in essence, a form of social entrepreneurship. Marketing, as well as informing and enlightening, showing what's going on. Consumers have responded to that. It started with a very small group of people, real flower power types: bearded men and sandal-wearing women; people who were willing to settle for lower quality for a good cause. Until well into the 1980s, fair trade products had a stuffy image and were available only on a small scale in Third World aid shops. You really had to be very motivated to be able to buy all your groceries "responsibly."

And yet, the tone had been set, consumers turned out to be

open to it, and more and more producers jumped on the fair trade bandwagon. Fair trade products became better quality and more interesting, tapping a new group of consumers: in marketing terms, these are referred to as early adopters, consumers who are willing to pay a premium for top quality. Thanks to the Max Havelaar quality label, it became easy for major producers and stores to reach these consumers and commit to "fair products."

Fair trade products' higher profile and social acceptance of these products prompted major chains to join the trend, one of which, Ahold, launched its own similar label called "*puur & eerlijk*" (pure and fair). It is safe to say that Max Havelaar's greatest achievement is that it has paved the way for that step from niche to volume.

seals that have washed up on the shore is something no one would question, but getting consumers on board to counter the harmful effects of climate change is far less straightforward. Consumers might even dispute the validity of the latter mission. Being served by a waitress with an intellectual disability is something many people find endearing, but by someone with a psychiatric "past or present," as at Amsterdam's exquisite Freud restaurant, is something many people find a little scary. A social entrepreneur therefore needs his or her cause to be popular, or at least understood. Is there anything he or she can do to make it so? Personally perhaps not, as that would focus too much attention on the social mission and away from the quality delivered, and that is counterproductive. However, there is a charity for virtually every social cause, and these charities could do the social entrepreneur's "dirty work" by raising customers' awareness to the problem. This would create a more fertile breeding ground for the social entrepreneur's solution.

This kind of partnership is interesting. Because what will you as an entrepreneur do whenever such an organization comes out with important news? What will Yumeko, for example, do when an animal rights group exposes new abuses in the poultry industry? That is the kind of news the company would like its customers to know about, as it raises awareness, helps fight the cause that Yumeko stands for. But Yumeko would not post this kind of news on its homepage, because it is too negative and activist, and would not prompt normal customers to buy a new comforter, it might actually put them off. They would, however, publish this news item in their newsletter.

A social entrepreneur faces a tough dilemma. Is he or she a merchant or a minister? Selling his or her merchandise is necessary, but at the same time the overriding aim is to win customers over to his or her goal. But a minister who imposes and nags, who only preaches, will not convert many people, his congregation will remain small. Being a good salesman is a prerequisite. Luckily for social entrepreneurs, the social undercurrent works in their favor — which is also the reason why the number of social entrepreneurs is growing — as consumers are becoming increasingly socially aware. That's making things easier for social entrepreneurs. Because even though the message is not yet lapped up like God's word by a church of hungry believers, social entrepreneurs aren't exactly speaking to deaf ears either. But it is often still a fine line.

In short, a social enterprise's mission has to be a factor in its marketing and positioning. You want customers to be aware of your mission and take it into consideration in the buying decision process. And the entrepreneur wants to make the world a better place by making customers more socially conscious and changing their habits. Your customers will, after all, eventually be the ones who make your product or service great, loyal customers can become ambassadors for your company.

Social says something about how people treat each other, and that also goes for the bond between enterprise and customer. That bond should be embedded just a little bit deeper.

Tony's Chocolonely: guaranteed slavery-free

It began in 2004, when TV journalist Teun van de Keuken stumbled upon atrocious practices in the cocoa industry as he reported on abuses in food production for his TV show. Cocoa producers in West Africa turned out to force children to work on plantations, unpaid, sometimes working 16-hour days. Children were effectively enslaved. Van de Keuken condemned cocoa farmers, producers, as well as consumers like himself: all are accessories to this abuse in equal measure. He even tried to get a judge to confirm his own complicity by turning himself in as a "chocolate criminal." When you buy a stolen bike off a junkie, you are committing a criminal offense, because you're handling stolen goods, and by that same logic you are also perpetrating a criminal act when you knowingly and willingly eat unlawfully produced chocolate. It got a lot of publicity, but no conviction. When Nestlé, the world's largest cocoa maker, openly denied the existence of slavery in the chocolate business, ignoring Van de Keuken's call for slavery-free chocolate production, he decided to rid chocolate production of slavery himself. At the end of 2005, he came up with the name Tony's Chocolonely (Tony after Teun, and Chocolonely because he felt alone in his fight) and had five thousand bars made, which he subsequently sold in no time.

Van de Keuken's goal is to change the chocolate industry through his brand, the publicity he generates, and the ensuing public awareness. And partly prompted by the Tony's Chocolonely initiative, Dutch chocolate maker Verkade announced in 2007 that it would only be using fair trade cocoa from then on.

A social enterprise that arises out of a TV show, it was a first in the Netherlands. It also gave the brand a flying start, so much so that the Dutch media watchdog threatened to impose a hefty fine for unlawful advertising — although the fact that it was an "idealistic product" constituted an extenuating circumstance. The brand is now run separately from the TV show, and Van de Keuken's role has been reduced to that of spiritual father of the company. These chocolate bars of highly acclaimed quality are now available in various flavors, and several spin-off products have meanwhile also hit the market, including chocolate sprinkles. In 2013, the company posted sales of 9 million euros, employed fifteen people, and was run by Henk Jan Beltman, an inspired entrepreneur with a business background and extensive experience in the food industry, who also holds the majority of shares.

Tony's Chocolonely very explicitly involves its customers in its mission. Not through advertising, because the company does not believe in advertising, but instead through social media and directly through its products. The product itself draws attention to the mission through its shape, as the bar is not divided into neat rows of rectangles, but into asymmetrical portions, reflecting the uneven distribution of wealth in the chocolate business. All in all, it is virtually impossible for buyers not to cotton on to the entrepreneur's mission.

And from a distance, Teun van de Keuken keeps weighing in through his TV show and his column in the *Het Parool* newspaper, aiming some fierce criticism at Max Havelaar and their fair trade certification, for example, which he considers to be not good enough: poor control of the origins of cocoa beans, late payment of already low premiums, and money flowing to the wrong places.

In July 2013, Tony's Chocolonely found a solution in the form of the "Bean to Bar" concept. Cocoa beans are procured directly from farmers in Ghana and Ivory Coast, with whom the company enters into long-term partnerships: Tony guarantees it will buy the farmer's beans for five years, while leaving it up to the farmer to decide whether or not to actually sell, because "that's how it should be between financially unequal parties." Benefits for farmer and Tony: the farmer is ensured certain sales at a good price and the chocolate brand knows exactly where its beans come from and that they are doing the right thing.

"We are living in a phenomenal age. If we can spend the early decades of the 21st century finding approaches that meet the needs of the poor in ways that generate profits and recognition for business, we will have found a sustainable way to reduce poverty in the world."

Bill Gates, founder of Microsoft, philanthropist

5

Ties and trust

Social enterprises' contribution to society

Economics was once a social science, but we seem to have lost sight of its social aspect. In the previous four chapters, it became clear that the social aspect is the common denominator, while the ties that arise are perhaps the greatest value created. "Social entrepreneurs excel at togetherness," says Sally Osberg, president and chief executive of the Skoll Foundation, one of the world's largest social entrepreneurship-promoting organizations. Social entrepreneurs seek not only a social solution, but fundamentally seek a joint solution. In this chapter, we will further zoom in on the connecting effects of social entrepreneurship, in numerous new forms.

Or in an old form. One form of social entrepreneurship that has never really disappeared, but only needed dusting off and ridding of its stale smell is that of the cooperative. The Netherlands' highest-profile cooperative is the Rabobank, now the largest bank in the Netherlands. Cooperatives were also very common in agriculture, one example being FrieslandCampina. The central feature of a cooperative is that its members are the owners. This is a highly democratic business format: the basic principle is that each member has one vote. In itself, this does not guarantee the benevolence of the organization, let alone that it automatically leads to social impact: a cooperative's focus could very well be limited to looking after its members' best interests, but these members' shared objective is unlikely to be malicious. It is therefore probably no coincidence that of all the major Dutch banks, Rabobank — although certainly not spotless — was the only one not to need a government bailout during the recent credit crunch. On the Dutch island of Texel, people are really into community finance. TESO, the ferry service to the mainland, is financed by the islanders as a nonprofit corporation, and the island is also home to TexelEnergie, a cooperative with major impact on the island's population.

A fine example outside the Netherlands is Mondragón, which is the name both of a small town in Spain's Basque region and of the umbrella cooperative that employs the majority of the town's population. Founded in the barren 1950s by an enlightened priest in response to the crippling poverty most Basques suffered at the time, Mondragón has grown into a multinational with sites all over the world and is currently Spain's seventh-largest company. Each and every one of its eighty thousand employees is a member and therefore co-owner, which gives them a say in the company's decisions and strategy. Besides manufacturing high-tech products, Mondragón also has its own bank, supermarket chain, and even a university. Tuition will cost you fifteen thousand euros, but you can earn that back by working for the cooperative. What is remarkable about Mondragón is that although this cooperative proved highly successful in the rural Basque region, it has as yet failed to properly take off in the big city, Madrid, where the company seems to struggle to connect with the population, perhaps primarily due to the fact that this kind of collaboration calls for a mentality that is easier to build in the Basque Country, Texel, and Brixton, all three of which are islands in a way. Acquiring this communal mentality takes time.

Community trust

The cooperative society is an English invention that dates
back to the eighteenth century, and today the United
Kingdom is still leading the way in new developments.
One version that has been flourishing for some years
now is the community trust, the community enterprise.
Often based in former school buildings or other premises donated by local authorities, which is where local
authorities' — highly important — contribution ends,
these trusts are for and by the community. The objective
of community development trusts is to improve quality of
life in a community. One example is The Selby Trust in the
North London district of Tottenham, where, in view of the
riots of August 2011, there's a lot to be gained in terms of
community regeneration. On a large site in the heart of the
neighborhood, you will find converted classrooms used
by small enterprises, training centers, workshops such as
a furniture maker, common rooms, a covered basketball
court, catering outlets, a car wash: the place is brimming
with activity. The site is visited by 1,500 people every day,
who really consider the trust their property. Although the
trust employs someone to run the complex, operations are
controlled by a board of trustees that is largely made up
of local residents. The Selby Trust has an annual turnover
of 750,000 pounds, of which it generates seventy percent
itself, while the rest comes from subsidies, and is currently
in the process of setting up a microfinance operation to
help fund even more local initiatives.

One of the features of a trust is, apart from the fact that
it brings well-being and social cohesion, predominantly
that it has an economic focus: the community is seen not
only as a group of people, but also as an economic system
of money flows that can be used to benefit the community.
"We are the glue that holds the community together," says

Buurtzorg: self-management skills

Buurtzorg Nederland provides community-based care services for twenty-three thousand people. They do so with a workforce of almost 8,000 people, who operate in six hundred and eighty self-managed teams. You may expect a large organization like this to have extensive support staff and a solid structure. But no, Buurtzorg Nederland is a fine example of self-management. Barely any management, virtually no hierarchy, and no more than twenty-one head office staff.

That this enterprise is having an impact is shown by the fact that Buurtzorg was elected the Best Employer of the Year two years in a row. After many years working in the care industry, managing director Jos de Blok concluded that things should — and could — be better! Community nursing staff are given the space to do their job well: they know what each individual client needs, give people some much-needed personal attention, know the community, and therefore manage to really connect with their clients.

It works. Clients are extremely satisfied with the service, mainly because of the personal bond they have with their carers, something that was a matter-of-course in the old days, but is actually discouraged in the "modern day" care system that is marked by mergers to create huge cost-oriented organizations.

"Self-management is allowing people to use their creativity," says De Blok. "Trusting them. The extent to which you are able to build a relationship with a client determines the outcome of the care, and when that relationship is good, you will be able to intuit at any one point what the client needs." And that goes a lot further than "eating, washing, and going to the bathroom." It is precisely that personal attention from someone who knows you, your situation, and your family that people appreciate enormously. Smart application of user-friendly IT is crucial in this context: the administrative side is kept to an absolute minimum and meetings are held online, giving employees who are spread out over the country in small teams a strong feeling of being part of the organization.

"I never expected the teams' willingness to take ownership and ability to organize themselves to reach this far," says De Blok. "I am now even seeing departments arise spontaneously, from the bottom up. And also, in terms of our public image, our teams are doing great PR, appearing online, on TV, and in newspapers on a local level. That is something major institutions normally do not manage. At our company, professional ethics have returned, as has job satisfaction."

For more information on Buurtzorg and the principles of self-management, please refer to the work of Frederic Laloux: www.reinventingorganizations.com

one of the trustees. "All kinds of different cultures come together here. They come to take courses, look for work, use day care facilities, but also to play football and get married. Our motto is visible everywhere: *Many Cultures, One Community.*"

Another fine example of a community enterprise is The People's Supermarket (TPS), also in London. This supermarket has around 5,000 members, of whom 450 volunteer there. Their work is not entirely unpaid, because if you volunteer four hours a month, stacking shelves, cooking, doing administrative chores, or manning a checkout, you get twenty percent discount on your groceries. The organization does not run on volunteers only, but also has twenty paid employees to ensure continuity. A nice detail: The People's Supermarket carries mainly healthy and locally-sourced products, which they have made cheaper than less healthy products. They managed to keep cigarettes out of their assortment for a long time, and only recently started selling them, because at the end of the day the enterprise has to keep its customers happy, and that sometimes means making concessions.

Dutch neighborhood enterprises

Although neighborhood enterprises are not yet a widespread phenomenon in the Netherlands, they are appearing in some places. In rural areas, for example, where villages are depopulating as facilities disappear and economic activity wanes. One example is the village of Hoogeloon in the Netherlands' Brabant province, where local residents have set up a care cooperative with a small nursing home to ensure the village's elderly with care needs are not placed far away from their home and family. It works, and is also a business: the cooperative employs a nurse, has a physician come in regularly, and has several volunteers. It seems to be a trend, a response to the impersonal upscaling that has prevailed in numerous industries over the past few decades and produced abuses — in elderly care, at housing corporations, and in other areas. Users of services had zero say in matters that affected them, and that has turned out to be were things go wrong. That's when people start looking for smaller scale, for genuine relationships, and trust. Especially in the care industry, being able to look each other in the eye is extremely important. An organization such as Buurtzorg (see page 76) shows how small can be the new big.

In the village of Elsendorp in the Brabant province's Peel region, residents have taken control too. At the end of the 1990s, young people in particular left the village, which had a population of 1,000, in search of better homes, causing the local supermarket to close and elderly care to struggle. Now, the local elementary school is the nicest in the region, there is a modern community center that also serves as a library and care center, while 53 new homes have been built. And that without government funding, although the village did rely on money from a European Union development fund and financing from Rabobank. All arranged by the residents themselves. The full extent of solidarity among residents became clear when one of the sports clubs was hit by a significant cut in its subsidy. Elsendorp's other clubs instantly decided to jointly absorb this cut, and also came up with a plan to find other sources of funding.

De Âlde Delte is also an interesting example: this nature preservation society in the northern province of Friesland, with sixty affiliated farmers, is active in the area of landscape management, tending to wooded banks and windbreaks. Trimmings and brash from the trees were used to set up a new bio-energy company that provides heating for a number of large centers in the village of Beetsterzwaag. Revenue from this energy business is used to pay for the preservation of the wooded banks. "We are extremely proud of this project," say initiators Frans Postma and Jan van de Lageweg, "but if we had known in advance what we would come up against, we may never even have started. Getting organized turned out to be very complicated. There was not a single sample contract for windbreak maintenance, shared exploitation of a stove, or heat supply to a rehabilitation center. And on top of that, we've had to go through ten permit procedures, not to mention the funding problems we've had to overcome. We basically had to reinvent the wheel. And we are now pleased to be able to make this wheel available to farmers who are looking to embark on a similar project."

Following the example set in London, Amsterdam also has a trust. In Amsterdam's vast northern district, which has long been poor and unpopular, three neighborhood enterprises have joined forces under the name *Trust Noord*. And with huge success: it has produced numerous initiatives, ranging from a small shop on the ferry to the center of Amsterdam and a museum, to a makeover of the Noorderpark, which used to be the domain of junkies and alcoholics and is now a cultural breeding place, with special pavilions that house small businesses and catering facilities, creating jobs for 350 people. Since 2012, *Trust Noord* also runs a microcredit fund, the *Trustfonds*. The district's housing corporations, the local Rabobank branch, Triodos Bank, the DOEN Foundation, and an anonymous donor have put a total of one million euros into the fund, which is further growing because residents can now buy shares, starting at ten euros each. These shares make a popular birthday gift in the neighborhood, also because you can deduct half the amount you paid for it from your municipal taxes. Furthermore, being a shareholder comes with benefits at a number of local stores. *Trust Noord* has had a big hand in regenerating the area, raising quality of life, much to the delight of the housing corporations, who are seeing demand for their houses rise again, and to the surprise of the police, who are seeing community relations improve. It is setting an example for other cities, which are increasingly turning to the northern district of Amsterdam for inspiration.

Urban farming is emerging in various Dutch cities, mostly as a private initiative in a neighborhood or community — ranging from broccoli grown at a former Amsterdam gas filling station, to radishes growing on fish manure in a hangar in Rotterdam. From large-scale to small-scale initiatives, from vegetable garden to acres on wasteland, in hangars and on top of office buildings, some are so extensive that they can supply supermarkets. Urban farming is, of course, nothing new. There have always been fruit and vegetable gardens in cities, used especially in times of crisis, but this current form is new, as they crop up at places that were not intended to be used for agriculture, such as roofs of office buildings. There are several benefits: urban farming brings huge savings on transport and carbon emissions, while also using premises that would otherwise be derelict. Plants decrease the overheating of the city and clean the air of particulates. And it is just fun to eat locally produced vegetables, even though it costs a little more than mass-produced apples, broccoli, and strawberries. It boosts social cohesion in the neighborhood: working on something together with your neighbors, digging up the soil together, and tending to crops together.

Connecting generations

As we pointed out at the start of this chapter, social entrepreneurs excel at togetherness, and have a great knack for constantly coming up with new and often joyful formats. We were filled with joy, for example, when we heard about a young company called Granny's Finest. Of the 2.6 million elderly people in the Netherlands, nearly half is lonely to very lonely. This sad fact inspired the people behind Granny's Finest to come up with an original concept. Our senior citizens like knitting, but have no one to knit for (as their grandchildren prefer H&M to granny's knitwear). And there are also young designers who have designed knitting patterns, but lack the time and funds to actually produce the knitwear they designed. Granny's Finest now brings these two groups together in knitting clubs (a bit like sweatshops, because it will undoubtedly be hot in there), where the elderly ladies knit the designs and are paid in excursions. They attach a card with a personal and, as you would expect, sensible piece of advice to each scarf, sweater, or woolly hat they knit, and buyers are required to send the maker a thank-you card. It is nice to know for whom you are knitting, and it is nice to know who knitted your sweater. This spreads a little happiness all around, and that's what it's all about in the end.

Het Goed: innovative recycling

A sweater with red and black stripes: €8.95. An Abba CD —
Super Trouper: €2.95. A pair of Nike sneakers, white-pink:
€14.95. A three-legged coffee table, nicely spotlit on a small
podium: €12.95.

Is it Macy's? Sears? No, it's a random selection from the
items on offer at Het Goed, a Dutch chain of thrift stores. Grub-
by, smelly, and full of other people's cast-offs? No. Although they
sell second-hand goods, Het Goed's assortment of clothes is
neatly organized by product group, on wooden hangers or in tidy
wardrobes. "Two people from our store layout and presentation
department learned their trade at IKEA. As a retailer, we are the
new kid on the block, and we're trying really hard," says Willem
van Rijn, managing director and owner of Het Goed.

Het Goed meanwhile has twenty stores, partly in a franchise
set-up, with a joint turnover of around 14 million euros from
sales to over 1.4 million customers — recycling is serious
business. And it is also a highly social business, because Het
Goed pursues a dual social objective: not only do they promote
reuse, they also employ people who are disadvantaged on the
job market. Of its eighthundred staff, a large part joined through
a work-study program. "Putting work into recycling" is their
motto. "We can find a suitable job for pretty much anyone," says
Van Rijn. "If you want to work up a sweat, you can ride with
our transport crew, picking up goods from the kind people who
donate to us. If you are good with people, you will fit right in at
our stores. If you like reading, you may like sorting all the books
we get in. We often get people who have got stuck elsewhere,
and to whom working at Het Goed is their last chance. At Het
Goed, they learn to work, but we are not a daytime activity
program run by the government, we are a business: they do have
to perform to the best of their ability."

For working with these employees, Het Goed receives a

supplement from the government. The state assesses someone's earning capacity and supplements that using funds from
various financial support programs, such as unemployment
benefits, welfare, invalidity insurance for young disabled people,
etc. And the recycling company also has dealings with that same
government in another area: the government pays Het Goed to
pick up goods that would otherwise be thrown away, and the
revenue they create this way adds up to twenty percent of the
company's annual turnover. "The rates the government pays are
under pressure, due to surplus capacity in the waste incineration
market. And the financial support we are entitled to for employing disadvantaged people is also not secure." Van Rijn chooses
his words carefully, as if he were trying hard not to speak ill of
an important business partner. "I'm used to a certain level of
changeability on the side of the government; whenever the local
council changes, we are at risk of suddenly losing our collection
contract (in a collection contract, the local authority agrees to
pay a certain party, in this case the recycling store, a fee per
resident in return for collecting items residents want to dispose
of). After all, each new alderman has their own plans. And each
new minister of social affairs introduces a new scheme, just
think back to the infamous additional job scheme for the long-
term unemployed implemented by one state secretary in the
past. But still, the way they are slashing budgets now is something I've never seen before. Het Goed is growing and turning a
profit, but times are hard. I see it as a challenge that is part and
parcel of business. It is forcing us to stretch the leverage we get
out of our customers, to be innovative. We have, for example,
also started selling certain items on consignment. And we are
doing up our stores to make them look even nicer. Look, this is
our lunch eatery at our Lelystad store. With used furniture, that
goes without saying. Pretty huh?" And yes, it looks sleek and hip.

Het Goed's headquarters are in Emmeloord, next door to
the offices of *Marktplaats*, and that is no coincidence: what is

now an online auction website, was once part of Het Goed. "In actual fact, that historic tie was also a disadvantage in certain situations. During negotiations, local authorities assumed we were awash with cash." In 2004, *Marktplaats* was sold to eBay for 225 million euros. Van Rijn worked at Het Goed at the time. "I was managing director then, and had been working at the company for a few years. I majored in mechanical engineering and environmental science, and ended up at Het Goed by pure coincidence. I started at the bottom." And now he's the big boss. "But I don't see myself that way, as the boss. I have final responsibility, true, but it's a joint effort. I've got good people around me, recruiting good people is my forte. I feel blessed every day to be allowed to be their manager." Is that kind of modesty typical of a social entrepreneur? "I don't know. It's typical of me." He prefers to show us round the sorting facility.

"This is where all textiles come in, our primary product group." This facility is about fifty meters long, with a long conveyor belt lined by around twenty women, sorters. The speakers blare out The Police's "Every Little Thing She Does Is Magic." Five large carts stuffed with clothes are ready at the start of the belt. Items of clothing from these carts are sorted on the conveyor, one sorter grabs a pair of pants, sweater, shoe and checks it both quickly and thoroughly, pulls on it, looks again, and then throws it in a container that will go to the store or a container that will go to the Salvation Army, which is where the rejected clothes go. "Sorting is the most difficult job at our company: everything that comes in is unique."

What about Het Goed's social impact? "That impact is great. On the CSR Performance Ladder, we are among the top fifteen in the Netherlands. By reusing goods, we save twenty thousand tons of carbon emissions every year. Our stores bring economic activity to difficult neighborhoods." According to Van Rijn, there is more the government could do to facilitate social enterprise. "One very simple measure would be to let us sell without having to charge sales or value added tax, which would be logical considering sales tax has already been paid on these goods in the past. What's difficult in dealings with the government is that their perspective is limited to that of the different implementing agencies, and they are not able to see the bigger picture. For every euro they pay us, they get more in return, a lot more. But most civil servants do not think in terms of investment, but only in terms of budgeting. Often, social gains are achieved on a level other than the level were investments were made. As income tax, for example."

His visible irritation evaporates as soon as we re-enter the store. "Just look how beautiful it all is! You know, there is still so much good we can do. I would like to be able to ensure even more that the people who donate goods to us know that their things end up in a good place. And involve our customers more, letting them know that they are doing a good thing by recycling, turning them into fans, perhaps even ambassadors. There is still a world to win."

6

To measure is to know

Quantifying social value

A social entrepreneur wants to change something in society, that's his or her primary aim. But while it is relatively easy for Unilever or Shell to quantify how many boxes of detergent or liters of gasoline they have sold, how much revenue and profits that has generated, compiling a social enterprise's bottom line is a lot less straightforward.

And yet, quantification is still something a social entrepreneur must strive for. He or she cannot get away with simply saying: "I'm doing good, so it's all good." He or she needs to know what exactly is good, whom it benefits and how. This is important for the entrepreneur to know in the first place. If social value is your mission, you need to know how to maximize that value. That is the basis of the operation. How can you reach your objective in the most effective manner? As soon as an enterprise has grown to a certain scale, the gratification an entrepreneur gets from doing good alone is no longer enough, that's when hard facts are needed. These will help the entrepreneur in communications, at least for motivational purposes — making sure everyone in the enterprise knows that what they are doing works.

A key stakeholder group is that of financial backers and potential financial backers, the impact investors who do not only consider financial returns, but also seek social value. We will cover them in greater detail in Chapter 8, but

Yumeko: change the world sleeping

Stephan Zeijlemaker (1962) and Rob van den Dool (1965) were having increasing trouble sleeping — and not only due to the eco-unfriendly production methods used to make their bed linens. Both were working in communications, owners of an advertising agency and an internet firm respectively. The level of satisfaction they got from their jobs was dwindling, and one day they decided they simply could no longer ignore that. And that was when, in 2009, the "yummy = eco" plan arose, which saw them start a new business in 2010 with the motto *change the world sleeping.*

Yumeko is all about ethical and ecological pioneering. This enterprise has stirred up and innovated the market through the introduction of the first ever fully sustainably produced bed and bath linen line, made with respect for people, animals, and the environment. Making the impact visible is an essential part of their policy and in substantiating claims financial backers and customers. Yumeko has chosen not to go down the route of monetization and adding up different impacts, but instead views these impacts alongside each other. It starts with the user market, consumers: the percentage of Dutch people who buy eco-friendly and fair trade bedding.

Anyone can read the Yumeko impact report on their website. In 2012, the impact was, in concrete terms:

- 6000 liters of chemicals saved, no artificial fertilizer used, no agricultural pesticides used, no chemical substances used in the fabric production process to bleach fabrics, no genetically modified seeds. This means less poison for farm families.
- 460 Indian families with a fair income.
- Millions of liters of water saved in the dyeing process.
- Thousands of animals treated with respect. No geese plucked alive for their down. Organic and local sheep

breeding and duck farm. Supervised by TNO (Netherlands
Organization for Applied Scientific Research) and NVWA
(Netherlands Food and Consumer Product Safety Authority).

Sleep softly, the world is hard enough as it is.

they too make investment decisions based on facts.

Being able to explain your results is also an essential requirement for marketing and PR. In Chapter 4, we
discussed the relationship with the customer, the value
added by the mission. But you need to be able to prove
that. Better yet, a social enterprise that cannot substantiate
its value claims opens itself up to criticism.

A number of methods

Internationally, impact measurement is a discipline that is
still in its infancy, lacking standardization, and you'll struggle to find an expert in this field, because there are very
few. Merely selecting a measurement method is already
difficult, let alone executing it correctly. Measuring impact
takes time and costs money, and it is in entrepreneurs'
nature to prefer to put their energy into building up their
companies. It has consequently turned out that integrated
impact quantification is not yet common practice among
social enterprises. The most recent survey among registered social enterprises in the Netherlands showed that
under half of respondents never really measured impact.
And most of the ones who do, limit themselves to a few
indicators and have no integrated approach.

And still, there are already several methods for effect
measuring available in this rather young sector of social

enterprises, all focused on the impact that a social enterprise is about. If your aim is to get as many disadvantaged people into employment as possible, one very straightforward impact indicator is the number of such people in your workforce as a percentage of the total workforce. This figure is an indication and helpful, but it does not tell the whole story about the value to the individuals or society at large. The real impact behind this indicator depends on the type of people, their wage, and the way they are treated. So more advanced methods are desirable.

One such method is SROI, Social Return on Investment (see textbox on page 92). This method is marked by the fact that it monetizes all impact, which means that all impact is expressed in financial terms, even when the impact constitutes soft values, such as a boost to employees' self-confidence. This method is highly valuable in the context of investment decisions, partly owing to the way in which values are quantified and interrelated. This facilitates comparisons between different projects. A young Dutch enterprise called Social Evaluator has captured this method in an online work environment, supported by a network of experts, making it easily accessible to anyone who wants to use it.

IRIS, Impact Reporting and Investment Standards, developed by the Rockefeller Foundation, is a method that primarily tries to establish industry-wide benchmarks. McKinsey & Co has set up TRAS!, a database and expertise network aimed at facilitating quantification of social impact. And the Kauffman Institute, a highly prestigious American foundation that seeks to advance entrepreneurship, has been investing heavily in finding the ultimate solution, that one method that measures and knows all impact.

At Tony's Chocolonely, they are taking impact measuring very seriously. So much so that they recently came up with their own impact quantification method, as they found the existing method to fall short. The existing method was part of the fair trade certification process, for which producers had to pay a fee, but it remained unclear what exactly the method measured. What exactly does slavery-free mean to farmers and their community? Tony's Chocolonely designed a code of conduct with fifty points by which suppliers and they themselves have to abide (for example, all ingredients must be traceable) and compiled an impact quantification method by cherry-picking from various available methods: parts of existing methods were merged with the MIDCA model, which sources local information in Africa. The main principles for the new method are to enter into a long-term partnership of at least five years with farmers to get better insight into developments, and secondly to allow independent and transparent auditing of the method: Tony's Chocolonely has committed to honestly and without reservations publishing the auditor's conclusions.

This doesn't come cheap: measuring impact and having the results audited is expected to set them back between 20,000 and 30,000 euros every year, but that is an amount that Tony's Chocolonely, can afford, and it is money well spent. After all, what do you prefer? Spend an amount to see what your investments, including the fair trade fees, are spent on, or spend a little less but learn virtually nothing about the value added? It's not even an issue for Tony's Chocolonely. Better still, they are convinced the transparency will lead to a more cost-effective method, as proper impact measurement will also provide better insight into how best to support the farmers. It could, for example, help you find out that they need more funding than you

How does social return on investment (SROI) work? In essence, SROI measures and compares the costs of investments to both economic and social gains. SROI is therefore a measuring tool that provides insight into what value a social enterprise creates for society, and expresses that value in monetary terms. Take the example of Specialisterren. Specialisterren helps autistic youngsters from welfare to work. An investment in Specialisterren yields the government hard savings, as these youngsters no longer claim welfare and start paying income tax instead, turning them from a debit entry into a credit entry in the government's accounts. Aside from that, a job at Specialisterren also has a social value, as it lifts autistic youngsters out of social isolation into a social structure, raising their self-esteem. All social changes Specialisterren brings about are measured through indicators to which a financial value is attached. This way, SROI monetizes not only "hard," but also "soft" impact. SROI provides insight into the social and economic return on each euro invested. Specialisterren's SROI is 2.4, which means that each euro spent on Specialisterren, regardless of where it comes from, yields society €2.40.

thought, or would perhaps be helped more by improvements to their agricultural methods.

You can't measure everything...

We don't have a preference for any one quantification method — as long as entrepreneurs measure their impact. And as long as they are transparent, showing stakeholders exactly what they have achieved. Or not achieved, as the case may be, because it's important to also face facts. If it turns out, for example, that the efforts of a company have got three intellectually impaired persons a job in one year, while spending two hundred thousand euros on their efforts, you might want to conclude that they have not been very effective, and that adjustments are required.

But there is, in our view, a limit. It doesn't make sense to measure impact down to three decimals; social entrepreneurs can also lose themselves in excessive measuring, consuming a lot of their valuable time, as the abovementioned methods are fairly complicated. Even though it may help in convincing parties of the benefits and success of their social enterprise, expressing social value in monetary terms will in many cases simply come across as too labored. Staff at the aforementioned Ctaste restaurant are not only blind or partially sighted, they are often also traumatized by losing their sight. The fact that they now have a job, for some perhaps even for the very first time in their life, means a lot to them. Suddenly, they no longer need help and can actually do something for others. And that growing self-confidence may just lead to someone like that deciding to go and live on his or her own, start a relationship, and fully participate in social life: out of care and into society.

How do you evaluate the happiness of someone who used to be excluded and is now contributing to society again? And how does someone's happiness relate to reduced carbon emissions? Even if you were to manage to capture this in monetary terms, you couldn't possibly use that information in an investment decision by saying: "OK then, we won't invest our money in the blind, because we can get better returns on air quality." The words of the great Immanuel Kant seem to have been spoken with social enterprises in mind: that which cannot be expressed in monetary terms is of value.

Triodos Bank: not your ordinary bank

Bankers are crooks. Money-grubbers. Peddlers of inane products that benefit only them. They have plunged us into a financial crisis. All of them? No, like Asterix and Obelix's village that so successfully resisted the Romans, there is one small bank that has preserved its integrity. And it's even a Dutch one. Triodos Bank. They steered clear of toxic assets, and therefore never had to take a haircut. They did not do bonuses, as these in their view do nothing but incentivize irresponsible risk-taking. The global financial crisis has not impacted on Triodos Bank, quite the contrary, they have welcomed 250,000 new customers over the past four years, and capital invested more than doubled over the same period, standing at over 9 billion euros at the end of 2013. Other banks soon started copying the Triodos business model.

Triodos is a different kind of bank, a sustainable one. The most sustainable bank in the world, in fact, according to the *Financial Times*. With sustainability being an increasingly hollow concept these days, the question is what exactly that tells us about Triodos Bank. It tells us that Triodos Bank invests only in initiatives that actively contribute to achieving a better society. "In three areas: environment, society, and culture," says Thomas Steiner, Triodos' Head of Communications. "It's a nice trichotomy: we've got people and planet covered, supplemented with culture, because good education and a rich cultural life make these first two go together better." The number three is everywhere at Triodos Bank. Starting with the name: Triodos is derived from the ancient Greek, meaning "three ways." "Just like money, which can come in the form of a gift, a loan, or money you use to spend. In other words, spending money, lending money, and grant money."

Triodos was founded by four men, an economist, a tax attorney, a banker, and a management consultant, in the late 1960s in a time of major social turbulence. Although they were no hippies, but decent fellows from sleepy Aerdenhout and Zeist, they did have ideals and felt money could be a force for good in improving society, contrary to many of their contemporaries who condemned money as the root of all evil. In the early years, before it became a bank, Triodos operated as a foundation that invested their investors' money with NMB bank, which was at the time still a regular and independent bank, getting their stakeholders healthy yields and investing any surpluses in enterprises such as an organic farm, a natural foods store, and a homeopathic physician who wanted to open a new practice.

And they also invested in an organic-dynamic diner in Amsterdam, called De Bast, which is where the bank, in 1977, encountered the man who has been its managing director for fifteen years, Peter Blom. There wasn't a bank in the Netherlands that was willing to finance De Bast, an anarchist hotbed. Blom, who was still studying economics at the time, turned to Triodos and got a loan, but also became so interested in the organization that he decided to volunteer at Triodos. Volunteer! At a bank! Mind you, Triodos had not yet formally obtained bank status — they were not licensed as a bank until 1980. "It took the Dutch central bank, the industry regulator, considerably longer than normal to grant a license that funny little bank with its weird views," Blom remembers. They would rather have seen Triodos become a cooperative bank, like Rabobank. "But we didn't want that: we wanted to be a normal straightforward bank, also because we wanted to see how we measured up against other banks."

They never became a normal bank, and not because they didn't offer a simple current account until recently. The Dutch central bank's doubts were understandable, in a sense, because which bank lets its customers specify a destination for interest earned? Triodos Bank does: you can have the bank donate the interest you have earned on your savings to charity. And at which bank do rich borrowers pay higher rates of interest than poorer ones? This was the case at Triodos, the exact opposite of common banking practice. The underlying idea was to make things as easy as possible for weaker customers. And which bank has been doing crowdfinancing since the 1970s? You guessed it, Triodos. It wasn't called that at the time, but that's what it boiled down to. Private individuals were asked to stand surety for a loan. Never one person for the whole amount, but as many people as possible for an amount between one hundred and five thousand guilders. It worked: it instilled a sense of responsibility in both borrower and guarantors. "Whenever things were looking like they could go wrong, we would rent a room to have a guarantors' meeting. These meetings turned into brain-storming sessions that produced creativity and plans that often helped turn the borrowing company's fortunes around. In the first six years, we did not have a single bankruptcy."

The bank kept growing steadily, and now has a presence in the Netherlands, Belgium, the United Kingdom, Germany, and Spain. With eight hundred employees and over 437,000 custom-ers. But no matter how well things are going, this is still a tiny bank with a balance sheet total of 9 billion euros in 2013, which is a pittance in comparison to fellow Dutch bank Rabobank's 550 billion euros. These figures are not an accurate reflection of the bank's impact: Triodos' social success is the huge follow-ing it has generated. Eco-investing is common practice now, with over five billion euros invested in eco-friendly projects in the Netherlands, but it all started with the listing of the Trio-dos Green Fund on the Amsterdam Stock Exchange in 1990. The Chernobyl nuclear disaster prompted the creation of the Wind Fund, which gave the development of renewable energy a tremendous boost. By investing one guilder per kilowatt hour per year, which in today's money would be an average of thirteen hundred euros, a family could erase their carbon footprint. Even without the tax breaks the government now offers for green investments, the Wind Fund was still profitable right from the start. Triodos currently has four microcredit funds, which are funds that finance banks or financial institutions in developing countries. This is another area where Triodos blazed a trail because many followed suit. Today, every self-respecting bank runs several sustainable funds and publishes an annual social report to declare that they don't invest in weapons and human rights-unfriendly activities.

Has Triodos become more normal as other banks have gone green? Have the two sides come closer to each other? You would almost think so: the Triodos general manager, that activist economics student, wears a suit and tie now. And drives an Audi A6. And has a 272,000 euro salary. "That is a lot, I know, but low in the banking industry. We go by the principle here that the highest salary we pay must not be more than ten times higher than the lowest," says Blom. But Triodos, too, is moving with the times. The board recently proposed raising dividends from four to seven percent — a move that was not welcomed by shareholders, who feared it would go at the expense of Triodos' social objectives.

"And yes, on the one hand we are indeed a perfectly ordinary company," says Thomas Steiner, "where people work hard. But the way we make our decisions differs from how many other companies do it. Our guiding principle is always 'to try to enhance people's quality of life.' In hiring new people, in choosing a supplier, or in assessing a loan application, we always factor in the effects on the planet, the people around us, and development opportunities. Granted, that might be a bit more difficult than what people are used to, and be something you have to learn, but it produces better quality decisions, more effective ones. We are relational rather than rational, focused less on mathematicizing a decision or checking off criteria, because that produces a false sense of security. When evaluating a loan application, the applicant company's economic condition is an indicator rather than the deciding factor, a good account manager will also listen to his or her gut feeling."

Triodos' success also produces a pitfall. "We have to be careful that we don't get an inverted bank run," says Blom, "with everyone putting their money in a Triodos account." The word goes that Triodos is rolling in it. "You have to be able to turn savings entrusted to you into loans, not invest them with other banks, because that gets you nowhere." The criteria are strict: we do not lend to companies that are over five percent non-sustainable, and neither do we lend to companies that stand in the way of the development of a sustainable society. And so Triodos is affected by the crisis after all: there are fewer initiatives that meet their standards.

Blom has a clear vision of what lessons his industry should draw from this crisis. "Ideally, the utility function of the industry, in other words retail banks, should be separated from investment banking activities, banks' investments, mergers, and takeovers. And it would also help if banks weren't listed companies, because that only incentivizes a focus on short-term gains." Musing: "ABN AMRO, one of the top three banks in the Netherlands that had to be bailed out and is now fully owned by the Dutch government, could serve a very important purpose, it could be turned into a bank that actively helps businesses become sustainable. They are such a large bank that they could have a huge impact. And it would put the Netherlands back on the map internationally, giving us a product to export."

It never ceases to be an exceptional story: how an initiative by four idealistic young men grew into a bank that changed the entire industry, run by a semi-anarchist who dropped out of college, but who meanwhile sits on the board of the Dutch Banking Association and is the second Dutch member of the prestigious Club of Rome.

"Social enterprise can be seen as the DNA for the new economic order."

Staffan Nilsson, President of the European Economic and Social Committee

7

Practice what you preach

How to organize a social enterprise

José Manuel Durão Barroso, President of the European Commission, put it very aptly: "Social enterprises are, by definition, social in their ends and means."* It means you do not only have an attractive social mission, but also seek to help make the world a better place through the way in which you intend to realize that mission. That is, in fact, the only way. If you have a genuine social drive, you inherently want to organize your enterprise in line with your values and principles.

How does that reverberate in the way you treat your employees? And what is your approach to the environment? And to your suppliers? Because if you squeeze your suppliers, they will squeeze their employees, and perhaps even turn to sweatshops and child labor. In the words of Marqt's Quirijn Bolle (see page 24): "We never sell below cost, because in the end there is always someone who pays the price."

These are the best practices of entrepreneurship that is doing well on all levels. Triodos is an example of that, a front runner. From their eco-friendly branches and the

* José Manuel Durão Barroso, President of the European Commission.
Building Responsible and Sustainable Growth — The Role of Social Entrepreneurs, Social Innovation Conference, Brussels, 18 November 2011

correlation between the highest and lowest wage, to their advisory board that has been empowered to take a truly critical look at operations four times a year and has a say in charting the bank's course: they're getting it right on all counts. Practice what you preach, that's the bottom line. But how do you run your enterprise to be able to do so.

We started this book with the definition of a social enterprise. In this chapter we will zoom in on the fourth feature: a social enterprise is social in the way it is governed.

A social enterprise:
1. primarily has a social mission: *impact first*
2. realizes that mission as an independent enterprise that provides a service or product
3. is financially self-sustaining, based on trade or other forms of value exchange, and therefore barely, if at all, dependent on donations or subsidies
4. is social in the way the company is governed:
   - the company is transparent
   - profits are allowed, but financial targets are subordinate to the mission, and shareholders get a reasonable slice of profits
   - management and policy are based on balanced joint control by all stakeholders
   - the company is fair to everyone
   - the company is aware of its ecological footprint.

Transparency

Social enterprises are, by definition, transparent. A social entrepreneur who truly pursues a social goal and shapes his enterprise in a social manner will want that to show. And, conversely, there is no reason not to show it.

Triodos is a good example in this context: they organize meetings with customers to let them weigh in on strategy and policy. And there are also customer days, which is when they invite account holders to come in and talk to employees from all echelons of the organization. In the U.K., Triodos even went so far as to organize events that let customers visit companies that are funded by Triodos, so they could get a first-hand idea of what the bank does with their money.

It is a misconception to think that transparency is limitless and about publishing every single figure in the newspapers. Transparency has an inside and an outside, and it is the inside that is actually the most important of the two, from which the outside ensues. In other words: are you honest and open toward your employees, do employees, for example, know how much each other makes? Also, on the external side, social entrepreneurs also have this drive to share expertise and experience to get others to buy into their social mission and speed up its realization. This creates a pleasant environment, as we have noticed at meetings in our industry. Contrary to our experiences in other realms of business, social entrepreneurs look to connect with others, learn from each other: "How did you solve this?" And: "Which supplier do you use for that?" They share, virtually unhampered by a fear of helping a possible competitor get ahead. That open attitude toward others inspires the kind of trust you need from customers, investors, and your community.

MyWheels: sociocracy as the key factor

Car sharing: although it has always been rare, there were people who would share their car with the neighbors by hiding their car keys under their doormats, so that a neighbor could help himself to their car whenever he needed to. Car sharing had not developed beyond that stage when Henry Mentink launched MyWheels in 2003. Besides, most people were still able to park their cars right outside their homes, and simply didn't see the benefits of car sharing. After starting out with six vehicles, Mentink now has several hundred, and not just any vehicles: for 2 euros an hour you can drive an impressive BMW Z3 Convertible or an Audi A2.

But there's more. Mentink: "If you can share a car, why not a company?" MyWheels' organization is sociocratic, which goes one step further than democratic: decisions are adopted only when no one in attendance has a serious objection. And seeing as MyWheels has three thousand members, they work with representatives who make decisions on their members' behalf. MyWheels furthermore wants its members/users to become financiers, creating a mutual interest, which further strengthens the organization. Members who invest in the company are paid back in "free" miles. This allows MyWheels to grow and add cars to its fleet.

Mentink considers this way of working to be the key success factor: "What's important, in my view, is that profits cannot leak out. A company is like the human body, when you let blood leak out, the body becomes unstable." His goal is a twofold one: sharing cars is better for the environment, but he primarily wants people to solve problems together. And therefore MyWheels does not impose penalties when someone breaches the rules, but will instead put the person suffering the inconvenience in contact with the person causing it, to get them to come to a solution together, fostering stronger community ties.

Profits are healthy

In Chapter 1, we pointed to the ongoing discussion in the literature about profits and profit-taking, with many stating that a social enterprise should be nonprofit. That is an understandable view, because what matters at the end of the day is the social objective, i.e. impact first. However, impact ensues from a company's operations. A company often needs capital to be able to grow, and that is where financial backers come in. They are among the stakeholders, alongside the entrepreneur, beneficiaries, customers, employees, and suppliers or business partners, who all expect reasonable remuneration. But what is reasonable when you put impact first, or, echoing an earlier line in this book, when financial objectives are subordinate to the mission?

One possible line of approach is the Community Interest Company, a legal entity format introduced in the United Kingdom. This legal form stipulates that 30 percent of profits can be paid out to shareholders, and provides a framework that social enterprises and their shareholders can choose to adopt, which to us is an interesting thought. Elsewhere, we are also seeing 50 percent crop up as the norm. Although norms do help sometimes, every company is different. Stakeholders will have to agree on what is reasonable, while possibly also factoring in classic financial parameters, such as an investment's risk profile.

Everyone is heard

At pure social enterprises, all stakeholders have a say in policy-making. A system of checks and balances is required, as shown in the last few years by the disastrous effects the absence of such oversight has had at banks and care institutions, for example, but perhaps most painfully at various housing associations — once founded as part of the Netherlands' social housing program. Tenants were supposed to have a say in policy to ensure oversight, but this never materialized, resulting in some chief executives claiming all powers for themselves. The key is to involve stakeholders in policy-making in a balanced manner, ensuring that all interests of all stakeholders and society as a whole are weighed up and anchored in the company's structure. We need to be able to call each other to account. This is something that is very normal to a social entrepreneur. After all, social says something about the way people want to relate to each other.

There are various fine and successful examples of this among social enterprises. MyWheels' sociocratic model is one, and perhaps even the most far-reaching form. Their members have a voice, a greater one than in a democracy, where the majority rules. In a sociocracy, a decision can be made only when no one has a well-founded objection. To prevent meetings turning into bedlam, part of the power to make decisions is bestowed on representatives. The concept of sociocracy was developed by Dutch social reformer Kees Boeke in the mid-20th century. A handful of companies has since dared to adopt this organizational format, one of them being Rotterdam's Endenburg Elektrotechniek, which has given its 120 employees an equal say in decision-making and always based on discussions. This format has been recognized, and it relieves a company of the legal obligation to install a works council for employee participation, because the sociocratic organization already closes the gap between board and staff.

In itself, sociocracy is a fine model, but there are also drawbacks and it is not suitable for all companies. Social organization of stakeholders and division of ownership is also possible within more common organizational formats.

What kind of division of ownership suits a social enterprise? Which legal form will anchor the social aspect in the governance model? The first ever legal format specifically intended for social enterprises dates back to 1991 and was introduced in Italy, the *impresa sociale*, which is a legal entity that explicitly pursues a social objective. It is fairly similar to a cooperative, which automatically offers a balance between stakeholders, provided they are members. But a cooperative is not automatically a social enterprise. Cooperatives are traditionally intended to serve their members, which is not the same as serving society as a whole. In the Netherlands, we are seeing that social entrepreneurs are increasingly starting to go back to the cooperative, but most are corporations and foundations, often a combination of the two: a corporation with a foundation holding part of the stock, hence guarding the social mission. In themselves, these formats are fine, but the articles of association of all these entities should really be different from those of pure commercial enterprises or charities. Principles of profit-taking and governance need to be laid down and anchored, preventing a situation where one of the stakeholders can unilaterally decide to take the company in a different direction. We are waiting for the Dutch government to also take steps and proceed with the creation of dedicated legal forms that make it easier for social enterprises to anchor their social mission.

Internet, which has proved a blessing for social entrepreneurs in many ways, has already created numerous new ways of involving stakeholders. Just look at how Linux and Wikipedia are built. Or take VJ Movement, which lets its members decide what news they want covered by video journalists and cartoonists across the globe. Thuisafgehaald is another fine example of an online platform, which gives stakeholders, amateur cooks and eaters in this case, room to express their opinion, submit suggestions, and rate the service. And then there are also initiatives such as the fledgling enterprises Konnektid and Enviu, which let stakeholders make the product or service themselves, meaning that they by definition have a say in the process in a kind of do-it-yourself organization. Konnektid revolves around finding someone online who can help you solve a problem offline. Enviu tries to develop business models for social enterprises through crowdsourcing — and has already brought together around eight thousand people in its community.

Fair and green

True social entrepreneurs want to go further than merely basing their own company on this model, they want to revolutionize the entire chain. Be fair to everyone. Ensure that everyone benefits from the activities they initiate further down the chain, simply because that's their disposition. This goes not only for social enterprises that have set socialization of the chain as a whole as their primary objective, as Tony's Chocolonely, Return to Sender, and Yumeko have done, it should also go for social entrepreneurs who work on a local level. Wherever possible, Fifteen and Ctaste try to use organic products sourced from local suppliers whom they know, and uphold fairness and ethics in these relationships. They keep an eye on ecological consequences, and try to waste as little food as possible. Fortunately, this kind of attitude is taking root more widely, as we are seeing numerous regular companies and institutions, inspired by CSR principles, go down the route of fairer and greener operations.

Social in ends and means — it initially seems like an additional task for social entrepreneurs, but the opposite could also hold true. Improvements in terms of transparency and internal commitment produce motivated teams with lower absence rates and better performances. Dealings with customers change from transactional in nature to relational, as we are seeing in the case of TexelEnergie, for example. Your customers become your biggest fans, your brand ambassadors, who take care of a large chunk of your sales efforts for you.

De Postcode Loterij: money spinner for charities

De Postcode Loterij (The Zip Code Lottery), which was set up by Boudewijn Poelmann and three fellow founders, is, after the Bill and Melissa Gates Foundation and the U.K.'s relatively unknown Wellcome Trust, the world's largest private donor to charity. Every year, numerous charities, social and nature organizations, and social projects receive a share, to the tune of 291 million euros in 2012, of the funds generated by Poelmann's lottery. This makes Poelmann by far the Netherlands' most successful social entrepreneur, which has taken him to high places, as evidenced by the photos all over his office of him rubbing shoulders with the rich and famous of this world.

His story is a good one, going back twenty-five years to when he started out with only six thousand guilders in savings, and not even his own savings, they were his wife's, and a small loan from Oxfam Novib, the international cooperation charity. Poelmann had spent ten years fundraising at Oxfam Novib, combining business and ideals — an unusual combination that suited Poelmann down to the ground. The charity's famous calendar was his idea, as well as the series of novels by writers from the developing world, and a magazine entitled *Onze Wereld* (which has since been rebranded as *One World*). When he subsequently became an independent consultant, many organizations turned to him for help: they all needed money, year after year.

Then what happened? "I actually got the inspiration from my wife's family, who are fruit growers. They plant a tree, water it, see it grow and bloom, and then yield fruit, and this cycle keeps repeating itself. I wanted to create a money tree, a perpetual money-making machine for charities. I thought of two possible kinds of enterprises that could do that: a bank and a lottery. I'm glad I went for the latter," says Poelmann, although he quickly adds, in a more cautious tone of voice: "But I'd actually still like to start a bank."

A lottery it was. The Netherlands already had a state lottery, as well as the Lotto and BankGiro Lottery, with the latter operating as per the same model Poelmann and his partner Frank Leeman had in mind. A large part of the profits would go to charity, but this new lottery would, contrary to existing ones, donate as much as sixty percent of its profits to charity. "To be able to succeed in the lottery business, we needed a participation format that was different from all others. After it turned out that using telephone numbers as lottery ticket numbers was not possible for technical reasons, it suddenly, and I remember this moment well, it was the middle of the night, hit me. I was woken up by a classic eureka moment: your zip code could be your lottery ticket number. Your zip code is something you share with your neighbors, so to get a unique lottery ticket, we added digits to the zip codes. If your ticket number is 4326 AA 01, your neighbor's will be 4326 AA 02, provided he or she also plays." A brilliant concept in many ways, so it turned out. The zip code-based system is inherently social, because if you win, your neighbors will win too. Provided they have bought a ticket, of course. And that is the flip side: people play out of a kind of fear of the neighbors striking it rich and them missing out. Although it might have been unanticipated, this effect has contributed considerably to De Postcode Loterij's success. "Granted, that may be the reason for people to take part," says Poelmann, "but those who stay loyal to the lottery appreciate the fact that we are able to support charities thanks to them."

The fact that someone's zip code makes them a winner, also automatically means that everyone knows where the winner lives. "That'll never work, especially not in the Netherlands, where lottery winners always opt for anonymity," critics said. Anonymity? Poelmann went the complete opposite route, not only clearly designating the winner and their zip code, but even having them appear on a TV show called *De 64 000 gulden vraag* (The 64,000-guilder question). "When you are new to a market, there are two things you can do: play according to existing rules, or make your own rules." The TV show turned out to be a stroke of genius, because being on TV makes you look bigger. "It instantly put us on the map. And our assumption proved correct: people find their one minute of fame more important than anonymity. Over the twenty-four years we have been running, it has happened only twice that someone did not want to be on TV."

But there was a lot more that made Poelmann's lottery so different when it first appeared, its prize structure for example. Other lotteries paid out modest top prizes, either because they were forced to or because they found that classier, while at De Postcode Loterij you stood a chance of winning a million. Given that this wasn't a completely risk-free strategy, they insured the top prize with Lloyd's of London in the early days. "Lloyd's of London always sent people over to attend the lottery draw, who would subsequently uncork the champagne whenever the jackpot wasn't won."

And like in any proper success story, there were also setbacks. Very serious ones, in fact: the company came very close to toppling when only fifty thousand participants were left after the first draw, and it was thanks to the Dutch postal service, which sent out three mass postal mailings for free, that De Postcode Loterij didn't die an early death. We had to allay the mistrust. "It came from the left and the right," says Poelmann, "and persevered until a few years ago. I must admit that I've always found that hard to stomach. On the right, they called me crazy, because 'if you are a real business, you have to make a lot more money from that lottery.' And critics on the left initially did not believe our social objective. Today, they are all on board, but the World Wildlife Fund was reluctant at first, as was Greenpeace, and eventually I got the Society for the Preservation of Nature in the Netherlands to join, although they specified all kinds of conditions. Free money, you might say. But it isn't like that: they feared that by joining such a commercial lottery, their reputation would be damaged, and their reputation is their most valuable asset..."

And once the lottery started growing, criticism focused on the way they recruited members, by phone or direct mail, using tactics that some considered aggressive. It did in fact lead to a penalty now and again, or negative press. Perhaps it is intrinsic to the essence of De Postcode Loterij: to be able to maximize payments to beneficiaries, i.e. charities, they have to — albeit while abiding by the rules — maximize their revenue in a competitive market.

In 2012, De Postcode Loterij had a turnover of 582 million euros, of which 291 million went to 89 beneficiaries. Every year, a large share of the earnings go to the DOEN Foundation, a fund set up by De Postcode Loterij as a facilitator for organizations that strive for sustainable, social, and cultural innovation. DOEN also invests in innovative social enterprises in the Netherlands and beyond. Novamedia has also rolled out this zip code-based lottery format to the U.K. and Sweden: The People's Postcode Lottery and the Svenska PostkodLotteriet.

De Postcode Loterij's social impact is immense; a considerable section of the social and cultural field in the Netherlands is dependent on the country's three charity lotteries. Could he ever have envisioned it would get this big? "No, I could only dream it. Within three years, we were already turning over one hundred million euros. It all went so fast. But I am unbelievably proud that we are having such a huge impact. I saw innumerable organizations doing extremely important work, such as the Dutch Council for Refugees, but never reaching full strength, either because they never made that breakthrough or because they had to put all their efforts into fundraising. We were able to help these organizations. And thanks to our scale, we can really make a difference. Energy savings, for example, is something we are pursuing. So we initiated a campaign through the lottery to hand out LED lights for free. Kleisterlee, the big man at Philips, heard about it. How many did we intend to give away, he inquired apprehensively. 'Not one hundred thousand, I hope.' No, I replied, two and a half million. This campaign introduced LED in the Netherlands. That is the kind of thing we can do, we have the power to make things mainstream. Such as the eco-corner that will soon be set up at Ahold stores. Because how do you get people to stop buying regular peanut butter and buy better-quality peanut butter? By making them have a good experience with that better-quality peanut butter."

Troublemaker, activist, Feyenoord fan in Amsterdam, marketing professional, entrepreneur, instantly available for the post of minister of Social Entrepreneurship ("You'll go crazy there within a week!" "Is that so? But I'm bound to also drive them crazy!") Boudewijn Poelmann. A week after we spoke to him, he emailed us the following powerful message: "Far too many future entrepreneurs never take the plunge or never make it beyond the start-up phase due to a lack of support, both financial and moral. But also due to a lack of perseverance or an inability to adhere to normal business practices and organization. It is hard to marry ideals and business, I know that like no other, but it is possible. I think the next generation is better equipped to do this than previous ones. Young people increasingly snub jobs in old-school industries in favor of something more meaningful. I see this phenomenon every day in our offices that are filled with happy faces and pride every time we pull something off or do something supernatural, like introducing LED lights into so many people's homes a few years ago."

8

Warm money

Investing in social enterprises

A number of years ago, Microsoft founder Bill Gates, with over 67 billion dollars the world's richest person, reported that he would go into philanthropy as soon as he could find the time. No one believed him. Today, Gates is one of the world's biggest philanthropists, pledging not only half of his capital to charity, but also managing to get other billionaires to do the same by signing The Giving Pledge. To Gates, money is not a goal, but a means to an end, which in his case is to improve health care around the world and fight extreme poverty. Pierre Omidyar and Jeffrey Skoll, founder and former president of eBay respectively, are going down a route that we like to see even more: they are using their wealth to support the social enterprise industry through the Skoll Foundation, which has since become the most important global force in this area. They work from a belief that this initiative will convert their money into something with maximum social value, the best-possible social return on investment.

But you don't have to be extremely wealthy to do good things with your money. To start with, you are a consumer who makes decisions about what to buy — or not buy — with your money every day. And the advent of crowdfinancing, for example, enables you to invest any amount in one of many (startup) companies that are looking to raise capital in this way.

Money, that's what this chapter is all about. Social entrepreneurs and money. At first glance, it may seem like a forced marriage, but social entrepreneurs use money to fulfill their mission. They want to make a profit to be able to have a sustainable and large-scale impact. As a start-up or when you want to propel growth, you need capital and need to connect with people who have capital to invest. But a social entrepreneur is not in it for the money, it is about his or her mission. And this is, of course, were there's friction. What financial backer will invest in a company that does not have making money as its primary aim? The entrepreneur needs to find warm money.

Return and social value

What return on investment can you expect from a social enterprise? If you mean financial return, and compare that to that of a "regular" company, we can be very clear: the risks will generally be higher, and it will take longer to recoup a financial investment. After all, the social mission comes first, and the entrepreneur will have a healthy inclination toward using the money to achieve that mission. For all fledgling companies, the first few years are filled with risk, but social enterprises grow even more slowly, which is mainly due to the fact that many social entrepreneurs enter markets that are still very underdeveloped (or were even created from scratch by them), and face problems that have not yet been solved by market mechanisms. So the risks are relatively high and the returns relatively low. Investing in a social enterprise requires patience, which is why this is often referred to as patient capital.

But even though returns aren't to rave about, Ashoka, the largest worldwide social entrepreneurs' network, still points out that investment in social enterprises has done nothing but grow over the past few years, showing that investors, too, appreciate social value. And yet, aligning investor expectations with those of social entrepreneurs is not always easy in practice.

Expected financial return on a social investment should, in fact, not be compared to return on a normal investment, because the social objectives come first. As a social investor, you have a say in a company that you connect with, you get a return on your investment and also create major social value. Compare it instead to a large donation to charity, which gives you zero return on your money and zero say in what the charity does with your money. Looking at it that way, you are a lot worse off than you would be if you were to invest and get shares in a social enterprise.

A social investor's primary reason for investing in a social enterprise should be to create social value, meaning that the investor must fully subscribe to the entrepreneur's social mission. Unfortunately, this is often still not the case, according to Ashoka. The number of investors who enter social value into the equation and want to put their money behind a social mission is still small, but it is growing, and it needs to for this industry to grow. Many investors' return expectations are too high and they do too little to find out what exactly the entrepreneur needs. Many still work on the basis of "the one who pays, decides," while that is not how social enterprises work. This has made social entrepreneurs shy away from potential investors.

Investors' role and input are important, and seeing them only as a source of money is unwise: if your investor were in it only for financial gains, he or she would probably have invested elsewhere. He or she is also — or primarily — in it for the social value. And that investors

PYMWYMIC: impact investing

PYMWYMIC is the acronym for Put Your Money Where Your Mouth Is Community, a social investment fund that was founded in 1995 by a number of men who had more than earned their spurs in the world of social enterprise in the Netherlands: Jan Oosterwijk (The Body Shop), entrepreneur Eckart Wintzen, Jan Willem Nieuwenhuys (ASN Wealth Management), and Frank van Beuningen (founder of the Gaastra clothes brand). Their most important investment was in the sustainable ice cream maker Ben & Jerry's, which has since been taken over by Unilever.

Nine years later, when all the money had been invested in eight companies (resulting in two good exits, three reasonable ones, and three fiascoes, which they euphemistically refer to as "involuntary philanthropy"), the set-up changed: Van Beuningen went it alone and initially turned PYMWYMIC into a matchmaking platform for investors and entrepreneurs in need of financing, and later into a social investors' club that currently has three hundred and fifty active members, all private individuals or families. Along with fellow founder and wife Margaret McGovern, Van Beuningen has invested in over thirty companies operating in the area of sustainability, health care, and food supply.

According to Frank, what is social investing? "Money must be put to good use. A subsidy is a one-off, that's money that disappears. Investing money means that you get it back and can invest again. And again. And again."

PYMWYMIC advises its members, matches investors to companies and vice versa, and (co-)organizes conferences and events in the Netherlands and the rest of Europe focusing on social entrepreneurship and social investing, such as SOCAP/Europe and the Impact Days. And things have taken off in a big way, says Van Beuningen. "The American bank J.P. Morgan projects the social enterprise market to be worth nearly 300 billion euros by 2015. It is also a market that large institutional investors are warming to. People with money in pension funds increasingly want to know what these funds do with their money. The economic crisis is helping us a lot. Investors who used to get yields of 10 to 15 percent are now not even topping bond yields of 3 to 4 percent. As a result, the companies in which we invest get a look-in. When you can get the same return on a social investment, the decision is a no-brainer."

expect a return is fully justified and wise. Investors will find some consolation in the fact that a well-established social enterprise has a lower risk profile than a regular enterprise, as shown by experiences in the U.K. Their strong bond with the social mission means that something really outrageous has to happen for a social entrepreneur to pack it in. Limited financial returns will never be a reason for a social entrepreneur to give up. Their long-term mentality makes them more stable, comparable to a family-run business.

Attracting capital

In most cases, capital is needed to get the enterprise started and enable it to grow after it has proven to be successful, and a large part of this capital carries risk. How much capital is needed depends on many factors: one start-up will only need a laptop and a good website, while another is based on smart but expensive technology, and sometimes a building or a piece of land need to be purchased for a store, warehouse, or factory. There are entrepreneurs with deep pockets or who use profits to fund growth, while others also need living expenses financed during the early phase when their fledgling company has not yet started billing customers.

If you lack the money and have to rely on others for capital, your first port of call is your direct network, those people who are close to the entrepreneur and his or her mission. Having taken that first step, new avenues will open up: government subsidies may be available, private investors may present themselves, and at one point borrowing money from a bank will also become an option. And there is also crowdfunding, a new option that has emerged online.

Friends and family are initial options, or the local community. If you cannot find an angel investor, you may have more luck finding a venture capitalist. Over 70 percent of Dutch social entrepreneurs invest their own money in their company.* This is, in combination with family and friends, an important source of seed capital in particular.

Most governments run schemes for start-ups, for growth financing, and some have specific funds for sustainable initiatives and public-private partnerships. The European Union has also set course in that direction, through the Social Business Initiative and investment funds. But tax incentives are also an option, as pioneered by the U.K.'s Seed Enterprise Investment Scheme. This scheme offers tax breaks that make it attractive for private investors to make social investments, thus helping social enterprises raise risk capital.

* Source: Social Enterprise NL Monitor

Impact investing

Impact investing, social investments by private parties in the form of a loan or capital stock, is booming globally. Impact investing is a form of investment that also factors in social value, and not only for social enterprises, but also for companies with solid CSR credentials. A broad range of parties have found their way to this market, varying from wealthy individuals and philanthropic organizations to financial institutions. The amounts involved also vary widely, both in terms of the investment modes and in terms of subjects, industries, and impact objectives.

Impact investments are investments that are intended to achieve a positive social impact beyond financial return. This means, among other things, that social impact is an important element, weighing in against financial risk and return. Impact investments differ from socially responsible investments (SRI). This latter form of investment is primarily targeted on minimizing negative effects on people and planet, comparable to CSR: do no harm. Contrary to SRI, impact investments actively seek to create positive impact. The concept of a combined social and financial objective is also known as the triple bottom line or blended value.

Paul Sullivan of *The New York Times* calls impact investing an "emerging hybrid of philanthropy and private equity."

> The Rockefeller Foundation and the Global Impact
> Investing Network, among other parties, commissioned
> the Monitor Group to assess the prospects for impact
> investing. Their 2010 report predicts a tenfold multi-
> plication of turnover, taking it from 50 billion dollars
> to 500 billion dollars. Impact investing is thought to
> have the potential of growing into one percent of total
> invested capital. This represents nearly one-and-a-half
> times the contribution of philanthropy in the U.S. — 31
> billion dollars — and six percent of the market share of
> socially responsible investments — 699 dollars in 2009.
>
> Source: Steven Godeke, *Investing for Social and Environmental Impact*, NYU
> Stern School of Business, 2012

PYMWYMIC, the Put Your Money Where Your Mouth Is
Community (see page 118), is a community of investors
that channels the flow of capital toward social impact,
playing an important role in building a strong segment of
private investments, so-called informal or angel investors.
They are also mobilizing family funds, banks, and private
investors, getting them to look into attractive impact
investments in the Netherlands and beyond. Committed
angel investors often invest with warmth. They also invest
simply "because they like it" — a great reason indeed!

Banks
And then there are the banks, those much-maligned
institutions that we expect so much from. It is understandable that banks set requirements when it comes to risk,
they have to work within a legal framework. The reality of
banks is simple: savers expect a reasonable rate of interest.
Banks generate that interest by investing the money that
has been entrusted to them, so they have to be careful.

Taking a lot of risk is not being careful. But still, they could do more, as part of their CSR policy for example. Impact investing and mission-related investing are high on the agenda at many banks, but this rarely trickles down to social enterprises. Ethical and green banks such as Triodos are leading the way and creating opportunities for companies with tried-and-tested models.

Crowdfinance

There is also a new way of attracting financing: crowdfinance, the form of crowdfunding that concerns loans or stock issues governed by the Financial Supervision Act. This involves raising capital from a large group of small financiers, mostly via the internet. Crowdfinance originated in creative circles: fans financing their favorite band's new CD — both new bands, such as through the well-known music crowdfinance platform Sellaband, and bands with a long history, such as the rock band Marillion. Today, whole movies are funded in this way, and Barack Obama crowdfunded his way to election and reelection. It is a young tool that burst onto the scene thanks to the unstoppable force that is the internet, but it has long ceased to be a mere hype. In places such as Silicon Valley, the breeding ground for tech start-ups, crowdfinancing is overtaking informal investing and is already a very common way for companies to get funding. Globally, crowdfinancing moves over a billion euros per annum, and it has also shown explosive growth in the Netherlands.

The Netherlands' biggest crowdfunding success to date was enjoyed by *De Windcentrale* last year: 7 million euros, raised for two windmills by 550 households, who are getting free electricity in return for the coming sixteen years. Their customers are more than just customers and the windmills are jointly financed. It is basically a very old

Wekomenerwel.nl: the generosity factor

Willem des Tombe, co-founder of Wekomenerwel.nl, knows from many years' experience at ABN AMRO that there are many potential entrepreneurs with good ideas. "Banks are not allowed to lend venture capital. And not everyone has an uncle or an aunt who can stand surety for a start-up loan. I have seen many a fine plan go to waste because of this. Innovation starts with start-ups. Crowdfinance should therefore be commonplace."

To many people, becoming a small investor in a start-up is still a major step. And most investors are not primarily in it for the interest or other form of quid pro quo. "The generosity factor often comes into it, especially when you know the project owner," says expert Gijsbert Koren of Douw & Koren consultancy.

For *Wekomenerwel*, that is exactly the secret behind a successful crowdfinance campaign: to tap into your network and build a community of backers. Investors often also become the first customers when the company gets going, and they also bring in further customers. Five to eight in every ten investors are (close) acquaintances. "This also enables you to gage your plan's potential for success," says Des Tombe. "If people from the inner circle of your network don't feel your plan is worthy of investment, you should probably pack it in." If the inner circle does want to invest, this will inspire confidence among people who are a little further removed from the entrepreneur or even completely unfamiliar with the entrepreneur and his or her initiative.

"Crowdfinance will spread to growth financing for SMEs and beyond, such as student scholarships and mortgages, creating a new business model where people arrange financing directly between themselves, without needing a bank or investment fund."

model with a modern twist. WakaWaka Power has raised over half a million euros from six thousand people through two platforms. Crowdfinancing is a form of financing that is perfectly suited to social enterprises: no other form of financing is so social and creates ties between people. As an entrepreneur, you must try to get your crowd to support you, and if you succeed and they invest in your company, they are often instantly also your best customers and most loyal ambassadors who will share their enthusiasm about their investment (and your company) with others. The Netherlands has a handful of platforms from which entrepreneurs can choose, all with names that reveal their youthfulness, such as *Wekomenerwel* (We'll get there), *Geldvoorelkaar* (Money for each other), Symbid, and Seeds.

In legal terms, crowdfinance is coming out of its infancy and has attracted the attention of the Ministry of Economic Affairs and industry regulators charged with enforcing the Financial Supervision Act, ranging from the Netherlands Authority for the Financial Markets and the Dutch central bank. Companies big and small can nowadays issue and market bonds, something that used to be very costly due to the legal, bank, and rating agency fees involved. Crowdfinance platforms often work with standardized agreement templates, which once they have been made can be reused by many others for a small fee.

Crowdfinance reduces the need to turn to family members, cap in hand. It creates an atmosphere of free choice, everyone is welcome. Friends can join in, or opt to stay out to avoid the risk of money matters spoiling the friendship. But there is also "generosity money": projects that are likable and humorous, while seemingly not likely to succeed in a business sense, often raise funds surprisingly quickly.

Social enterprises and money, the forced marriage... There is still plenty of room for development in that relationship. The pace is yet to pick up, but the opportunities are there. At family funds and large philanthropists, for example, who are jointly sitting on several billion euros that are currently kept by banks or tied up in very conservative investments. We hope part of that money will be used for investments with the same objectives as their philanthropic mission. And we also hope increasing numbers of private individuals, funds, banks, and governments will consider investing in social enterprises, and start looking at how they can use their capital to achieve a greater social impact.

"In the years to come, I believe we will see more social enterprises, making greater strides towards social justice, working more easily with conventional businesses and the public sector. We will see social enterprises thrive."

Tony Blair, former Prime Minister of the United Kingdom of Great Britain and Northern Ireland

Landzijde: common sense

Standing in an informal queue by a small table, a Caribbe-
an-looking fellow with gray dreadlocks, a man wearing a track
suit, and a cheerful woman who has a few teeth missing. A
motley crew, not the kind of people you'd expect to see on a
farm.

Plenty of smokers too, the barn air is blue with cigarette
smoke. Then a woman enters the room, carrying a folder and a
money box, and the hum of voices dies down, the queue forms
by the table. The woman takes a form from her folder, writes
something down, takes ten euros from her money box and gives
it to the first person in line, who subsequently carefully folds it,
puts it in his back pocket, and leaves. Next!

Jaap Hoek Spaans looks on approvingly. "They've worked hard
today, they have plucked and packaged a total of six hundred
kilograms of red peppers for La Place, one of *Kwekerij Osdorp*'s
biggest customers." This market garden is a care farm, which
is a truly exceptional phenomenon. A care farm grows vegetables or breeds cattle, while also being a daytime activity center
for around ten to fifteen thousand people in the Netherlands,
people with a mental disability, psychological problems, addicts,
problem youngsters. *Kwekerij Osdorp* is part of Landzijde, a
fast-growing partnership of nearly one hundred care farms in the
province of North Holland, of which Hoek Spaans is the chair-
man, the chief farmer. "Do you know what the best thing about
it is? This is their company. That's how they see it. Four times a
week, they are picked up by a minibus, sixty men, a few women,
of all ages, to come and work here. Some have been coming
here for a year already, others several months, some suddenly
don't show up for several months, because they're doing time.
There is suitable work for everyone, and you know what, these
guys know exactly when they are doing something useful or are
just being kept busy. They are proud of those ten euros they get

at the end of the day, because they've really earned it. And it is often a welcome top-up: when you are in a debt management scheme and you get thirty euros a week to spend, you can double your income here. 'I'm valued here,' I sometimes hear them say. While they are here, they are not people in need of help, but instead able to do something worthwhile. Yes, also for others. It's a huge boost for their self-esteem."

Hoek Spaans is tall, has a big head, and large hands — he looks just like you expect a farmer to look. "And do you know what this leads to?" He does not await my answer. "These people experience that they can do a lot more than they thought. And, after having worked for us, they find jobs at a bakery, the local authority, or in the kitchen of a care institution. Take that man over there, the man with the beard, he came in as a client and now drives the minibus to pick people up. But even when they don't move on to bigger and better jobs, the work they do here does them a lot of good: the boys become more patient, take better care of themselves, become less aggressive, cook for themselves more often, drink or steal less."

The figures are good. The government draws on various welfare budgets (Exceptional Medical Expenses Act, personal budgets, resources of the employee insurance and welfare administration) to pay for the daytime activity program, but Ernst & Young and the Trimbos Institute worked out in 2012 that these funds spent on a care farm are equal to how much the government would otherwise have spent on welfare for the same people, while the returns are far greater in a range of areas. Not only in terms of well-being — immaterial and therefore too often not factored in — but also improved school attendance rates, and with that better school performance, fewer junkies on the streets, and therefore less police involvement.

How are relations with the government? "Fine," says Hoek Spaans, "Amsterdam has had a policy rethink and now active-ly seeks partnerships with social enterprises. So our conifers will, hopefully, soon grace the city's public gardens." But the city authorities are most important as a supplier of clients. "We submit an offer, the city approves it and says: you are cleared to have people work under your supervision, and subsequently social services refers people to us. The next step is an intake at the client's home, following which we assess where this person will fit in best, and then it's off to work." Just like that? And what about counseling? Do you adhere to a certain methodology? Hoek Spaans frowns. "Our methodology is called common sense. You will not find a team of psychologists monitoring the place here. But there is, of course, professional guidance. Half of these counselors come from an agricultural background, the other half from the care industry, and they all excel at empathy. During the day there is always a moment when a client's particular problem surfaces, and that's ok. There is always room to talk about it, and not in some stage-managed session environment or in half-hour slots, but at a time that suits the client. The chance that the client will be receptive to counseling is then a lot greater: he or she has, after all, asked for it."

Would the care farm be able to survive without government subsidies? "No," says Hoek Spaans. "Our clients do the very best they can, but they are less productive than, let's say, a group of Polish or Czech workers. If only you knew how many cartons of milk our clients consume in a day. And I spend about 100,000 euros a year on keeping the place warm. It's a challenge. La Place (a chain of self-service restaurants) will not accept rotten red peppers just because we are a care farm. We have to deliver products that are up to current market standards using employees who are not up to current market standards. And we can only do that when people feel they are doing their best for their own company. We are in the green," says the farmer with a Freudian slip, "but we reinvest the money we make." In upgrading our kitchen, installing under-floor heating in the workers' lounge. Or in a new classroom: clients can get Dutch classes if they want. "But the look of the place has to stay a bit farmy, not too slick." And outside there's a full hectare of gardens, which is where fruit trees will go and a festival will be organized for the local community.

"When I lived in Purmerend, there was this local character called *Schorre Jan* (Hoarse Jan). He would cycle through the village at a very slow pace, one buttock leaning on the saddle, back stooped, stinky cigar in his mouth. Catching moles was his line of business. He would also regularly come to our farm to catch a mole or do chores in exchange for milk or bacon. Every day, he would go to another farm, and that is how the village took care of him. That's when the seeds of this idea were sown, as I saw how a farm and care can go hand in hand." Because, although Hoek Spaans comes from a long line of farmers, he initially chose a completely different career: he taught Dutch and geography at a high school, while running his organic dynamic farm in Purmerend was merely a hobby. "I devoted myself to rural innovation, launching the *Mijn Boer* (My Farmer) brand for locally produced products, which later became the Sligro super- market chain's sustainability quality label. I wanted to involve people in the farm, recreation would also have been a way of doing that. No, care agriculture was not an obvious choice. What I initially heard about it did not sound good. Too much hugging, too much 'look at my little farm helpers.'" That is clearly not the way they work at Landzijde. "Do you know what's also great? That it is making young people excited about becoming a farmer again. These young people initially saw their parents struggle and said to themselves: that's not for me. But like this, working with people, yes, this is how I want to farm!"

9

Hands off, support, or control?

The role of government

Social enterprises are strange things. They carry within them two seemingly incompatible concepts: "social" and "enterprise," how on earth can these go together? Isn't there the private sector, the market, on one side, and the government, the public sector, on the other? That is the classic dichotomy that is echoed in the words of Paul Martin, former Canadian Prime Minister, in an inspiring speech about social enterprises:* "Over the last 150 years, there has been a never ending debate between those who espouse the free market on the one hand and socialism on the other. It is clear now that the free market has won out — and it has won out because, at its core it gives full flower to individual ambition and entrepreneurship. It is not the free market in pure form that has emerged triumphant. The fact is, all developed countries depend heavily in one way or another on government for the delivery of public goods: universal primary and secondary school education, and public infrastructure, to cite only two examples. Thus, few would deny today the importance of the state in providing the social inputs that enable the modern economy to grow. What is less well recognized however is the contribution made by another building block in our social and economic structure — the civil society, which plays

* Speech Paul Martin, *Unleashing the Power of Social Enterprise*, 2007

an essential role in dealing with the unacceptable gaps in equality which arise from an intrinsic disadvantage or often from the fall-out of the free market."

In his 1776 book entitled *The Wealth of Nations*, Adam Smith, founding father of capitalism and free-market thinking, warned that the effectiveness of the free market mechanism hinges on close social commitment from entrepreneurs. Smith claimed that entrepreneurs must be out to create wealth for all fellow citizens, and therefore feel responsible for well-being across the whole of society. That's nothing new, that's social entrepreneurship...

Eckart Wintzen on value added

The late Eckart Wintzen, a progressive entrepreneur and corporate social responsibility pioneer in the Netherlands, said in a 1993 speech to managers at Shell: "The principle that underlies our economy is a fairly simple one. You buy something, add value to it, and sell the end product for more money than you initially spent. There's nothing wrong with that in itself, but we are not consistent in applying the rules. We are not settling the bill we're running up with our planet. Neither when we extract the resources we need from the earth, nor when we put our waste back into the earth. To keep it relevant to your line of business: you add lead to gasoline, which ends up in the atmosphere in a highly diluted form. In the long run, this will reduce the quality of the planet. That's an expense you are not paying, which basically makes you contraband merchants — and me, as your car-driving customer, a receiver of stolen goods. We currently tax value added, and that value is added by people. Nearly all taxation is somehow staff-related. Seeing as the system barely taxes material, we are seeing a proliferation of machines. And at the end of the ride, we are left with two problems: huge unemployment and an environmental problem."

Wintzen came up with a solution: instead of value-added tax, there should be value-extracted tax. His perspective on value and economy is an inspiring one, as well as one that suits social entrepreneurs. Unlike regular entrepreneurs, social entrepreneurs are not primarily in the business of creating financial value, but instead of creating social value, in other words real value.

Governments on the defensive

In the Netherlands, the private and the public sector are not as far removed from each other as they are in Anglo-Saxon countries. Or rather: they weren't, because things have changed over the past sixty years. Our society is built on private initiative. The old and major social institutions, such as the Red Cross, Humanitas, the Stedelijk Museum of modern art in Amsterdam, housing associations, schools and universities, are all the product of private initiatives from before World War II. The current dominant role of government in society is something that started after the war, when many of those pre-war private initiatives were (semi)nationalized and many foundations and cooperatives that used to run under their own steam became fully dependent on the government for policy and funding, and were bureaucratized.

Over the past few decades, the Dutch government has been trying to mobilize the power of the market and take a step back, a move that was recently accelerated by the economic crisis. Concurrently, with the government's retreat, social problems have increased, as we outlined in the introduction: the welfare state, which already struggled to provide structural solutions to many social issues, also weakened.

Management guru Michael Porter propagates the idea that the gap between government and business needs closing and says that striving for shared value is the way to go. "Companies need to reconnect their own success with social progress," he says. They need to beware of getting stuck in a "social responsibility" mind-set in which societal issues are at the periphery, not the core. In his often-quoted *HBR* article "Creating Shared Value" (2011), Porter writes: "A whole generation of social entrepreneurs is pioneering new product concepts that meet social needs using viable business models. Because they are not locked into narrow traditional business thinking, social entrepreneurs are often well ahead of established corporations in discovering these opportunities. Social enterprises that create shared value can scale up far more rapidly than purely social programs, which often suffer from an inability to grow and become self-sustaining."

In our country, increasing numbers of people are dropping below the poverty line, our education system turns out to be less able to get youngsters qualified, and immigration keeps rising, which is actually a development that is badly needed to stem population aging, but also produces new social issues. And on top of all that, the Netherlands also faces environmental and ecological issues that go beyond its national boundaries.

Or, in the words of the former Dutch Prime Minister Jan-Peter Balkenende:* "Companies are on the offensive, governments on the defensive. That is, in a few words,

* Prof. J.P. Balkenende, "Publiek-privaat in een nieuw perspectief" (Public-private in a new perspective) (2012)

the current situation in the area of social problems. Where business is proactively taking on sustainability, and where social enterprises are assuming a more market-based perspective on social issues, we are at the same time seeing governments trying to come to grips with financial problems, the need for substantial spending cuts, unpopular reform, short-term considerations, and populist sentiment. The public domain is partly falling into private hands."

Simplified: social problems have become bigger, but those who are supposed to solve them are less able to do so. The stars are aligning for further growth of social enterprise, that odd hybrid of a social heart and a business mind: Is it a charity? Is it a business? Is it a bird? Is it a plane? It's a social enterprise.

The fact that the government does not have a solution to certain social problems is in most cases also down to inability rather than unwillingness. New solutions are needed, and these require creativity and innovation, which happens to be where social enterprises come into their own: where the government weighs up interests, has to carefully make decisions, and walks that fine line between preserving the status quo and pursuing change, a social enterprise can act quickly, flexibly, and non-bureaucratically. Where governments deliberate, social entrepreneurs act. Social entrepreneurs are able to quickly adapt to changing circumstances or tap new opportunities.

Whenever the government wants to achieve something, they will often use the tool of legislation. To get people who are occupationally disadvantaged into employment, for example, the government can force companies to hire a certain number of such people. This comes with certain limitations, as we have seen in similar cases: whenever companies are unable to meet this kind of government-imposed obligation, they simply pay a fine and be done with it. The result: a form of additional taxation and the people the government sought to help are still sidelined. But a social enterprise such as Specialisterren does succeed, albeit still only on a small scale, where the government failed: they are helping autistic people get a meaningful job. Or take the minimum wage, intended to guarantee that people with a weaker position in the labor market can earn a wage they can live on, above the poverty line. Not everyone is able to earn this minimum wage, such as former inmates who cannot find a job or people with Down syndrome, to name only two very different groups with reduced earning potential. Without additional welfare schemes, people who are not able to produce the required output to merit the minimum wage will remain on the sidelines. Social enterprises often offer disadvantaged people employment, giving them both self-respect and economic value, even when these employees cannot produce the output for a minimum wage. The positive fallout of this is a reduction in welfare and care costs, and the rest of the population having to pay less taxes and premiums: the Netherlands Inc. benefits. Needless to say, there is a limit to this, because a social enterprise still has to compete with regular businesses, but that is precisely where the government can step in, by introducing compensatory and generally applicable schemes.

Big Society

Governments would like to see more social enterprises, not in the least because they realize these do important work for them. Barroso, the President of the European Commission, recently expressed the expectation that social enterprises will make up ten percent of the European economy in the short term: "The main objective of social businesses is to generate significant impact on society, the environment, and the local community, and their key aim is to effect social and economic transformation which contributes to the objectives of the Europe 2020 Strategy." There are currently, according to EU figures, already around two million social enterprises, employing 14.5 million people.

To back Barroso's words up with action, the European Commission launched the Social Innovation Europe platform in March 2011, which is intended to connect all possible stakeholders in this area and thus create a "dynamic, entrepreneurial, and innovative" Europe. And in October 2011, this was followed up with the Social Business Initiative, which has three main objectives: to introduce measures to improve social enterprises' access to financing, to raise the profile of social enterprises, and to improve the legal environment of social enterprises (source: European Commission on the Social Business Initiative). In the meantime, a Social Investing Impact Fund and a Social Impact Accelerator have been added, and work is going into legislation regarding Social Cohesion Policy and to improve access to the European tendering process.

For over a decade, successive U.K. governments have been working to embed social enterprise in the U.K. economy, initially under the stewardship of Tony Blair's Labour Party, which was attracted to the social element and the facilities social enterprise creates. The current coalition of Conservatives and Liberal Democrats has enthusiastically continued this process under the Big Society policy. The stated aim is to create a climate that empowers local people and

The U.K. Big Society

The Big Society policy includes a bank – Big Society Capital – capitalized by the injection of GBP400 million in confiscated unclaimed funds that were sitting in dormant bank accounts, plus GBP200 million from the major British banks, which will be used to finance social enterprises. And they also set up the Big Society Network, an ambitious platform that will support social enterprises everywhere.

According to estimates by the U.K. government, there are around 70,000 social enterprises in the U.K., which together contribute GBP24 billion to the economy and employ 1 million people. Recent British data (Social Enterprise UK, July 2013) shows that 39 percent of all social enterprises are based in the country's least prosperous communities, compared to 12 percent of all small and medium enterprises. A third of all social enterprise start-ups originates from the country's poorest areas.

Over 52 percent of social enterprises offer employment to disabled people. Across the whole of the United Kingdom, one in seven social enterprises is a start-up, over three times the number of start-ups among regular small businesses (14 percent against 4 percent). Social enterprises are twice as likely as regular companies to post a profit at the end of the year, and are more often run by women (38 percent), young people, and people from ethnic minorities.

communities, building a "big society" that will take power
away from politicians and give it to the people. The Times
described the policy as "an impressive attempt to reframe
the role of government and unleash entrepreneurial spirit,"
inspired perhaps by the success of the aforementioned
development trusts. "The Big Society is about changing
the way our country is run," said Prime Minister David
Cameron.

What governments can do

Promoting the development of social enterprises can result
in short and long-term gains for public budgets through
reduced public expenditures and increased tax revenues
compared with other measures of addressing social needs.
Social enterprises can also often be more effective in meeting public goals than either purely private or purely public
sector actors because of their local roots and knowledge
and their explicit social missions. Putting in place policies
that provide an enabling eco-system for social enterprises
is crucial if these businesses are to fulfill their potential.*

The above conclusion is drawn in the social entrepreneurship policy brief of the European Union and the Organ-
isation for Economic Co-operation and Development.
The brief notes some key areas of policy directly aimed at
growing the sector:

- Promote social entrepreneurship. Today, more often
  than not, the concept is not understood, which
  hampers the commitment of all types of stakeholders, from financiers to customers, from employees to
  governments. For the sector to flourish, it is a simple

* OECD/EU policy brief on social entrepreneurship 2013, European
Commission, ISBN 978-79-25428-4. www.oecd.org

prerequisite that people understand the mission and model of the social enterprise. Needless to say, this is first and foremost the responsibility of the industry itself, but it would help a lot if governments were to support this by providing a "stamp of approval," as we have seen in the U.K. Governments can do more, such as encourage academic research and education.

- Build an enabling legal, regulatory, and fiscal frame-
  work. Many countries have created a legal entity format that incorporates a social goal in a form that fits their culture. Italy was the first country in Europe to do so, opting for a variation on the cooperative at the end of the twentieth century. The U.K. followed with the Community Interest Company, the CIC, a variation on the Ltd form. These are entities that reflect a new way of thinking, that put social mission first, like foundations and public bodies do, while also allowing for a form of private ownership at the same time. A new paradigm that crosses the chasm and puts the owners in a new perspective, one of not primarily pursuing their own self interest. These entities come with restrictions of a statutory nature, and in the case of the CIC with a cap on dividends that demands them to plow most profits back into the public good while still allowing the investors a return. This legal entity paves the way for fiscal stimuli, as we see in Germany for social enterprises that create jobs for disadvantaged people.
- Provide sustainable finance. Many governments from the U.K. to Poland have created funds for social enter-prises. Some are directly aimed at the social enterprise sector, others are more co-investment schemes that top up private investments, thus decreasing private risk.
- Support access to markets. Governments and related sectors are large buyers of products and services. They

can help create a level playing field for social enterprises by valuing their social contribution, both in the area of people and in the area of planet. Instead of going down the route of "positive discrimination," they should recognize the actual value created in full. Legislation that stimulates the private sector in this way would obviously also be helpful.

These measures would help, but there is more to do, which can relate to all sorts of policies. To name a few:

- Governments can incentivize the provision of capital by innovating financial laws and opening up more space for new community-based forms of finance, like crowdfunding and credit unions
- Germany has shown that the renewable energy agenda can be based on private initiative, as it has removed barriers for energy cooperatives from energy and fiscal legislation
- The social enterprise sector in the U.K. has a large number of enterprises that operate in the realm of care, embedded in local communities. This is driven by a process of allowing communities to take control, and by public spinoffs. The Dutch social enterprise industry is home to a hallmark system-changing organization in Buurtzorg and an innovator like Zorgvoorelkaar, but offers little more. Care is still completely provided by huge government-controlled institutions where cost control is the primary management principle, resulting in low service while not meeting affordability objectives. Developing social enterprises in care also requires scrapping of typical control-oriented care regulations.
- The level of labor participation of disadvantaged people differs per country based on the measures a country has implemented to encourage the work integration

social enterprise. Germany, for example, applies a low value-added tax rate as a way to provide a level playing field for its *Integrationsfirmen*, compensating for the productivity disadvantage and higher training and management cost of the workforce with a tax break.

China

The social enterprise movement in Europe is eminent and broadly supported, but the form and focus differs by region, also driven by government behavior. While working on this book, we could not put aside our curiosity about the global applicability of its values and principles, where China is the most obvious real test. Is this a logical list? Confucius, Chiang Kai-shek, Mao Zedong, Social Entrepreneur? Will social enterprises arise in a society where "social" meant government and "entrepreneur" was not in the dictionary?

The 2013 independent report "China Social Enterprise and Social Impact Investment Development Report" opens with a familiar sounding statement: Social Enterprises, A Calling of our Time. Over the past few years, an increasing number of commercial entrepreneurs are no longer satisfied with pure economic returns. Instead, they hope to achieve significant social impact by using commercial means to address social issues.

The report provides some best practices that reflect China's societal issues. V-Roof develops roof gardening as a very meaningful social solution in China's polluted cities, helping to build the social fabric that is missing due to the enormous influx of people.

Boxue is a self-sustaining ecological village. Buy42 reuses and redistributes luxury goods using disabled employees and applies a one-for-one concept. Zhihui Elderly Health Care Cloud Service Platform provides internet technology-based solutions for elderly care.

In the domain of labor, China has a structure that has a striking resemblance to the German *Integrationsfirmen* approach, complete with a legal entity, "the welfare enterprise," and a lower value-added tax rate. You would almost suspect the Chinese have made study trips...

Not surprisingly, the social enterprise movement is just emerging, largely driven by young people who start to see the environmental problems and who see poverty and disadvantages, and who feel called to action. But all the signs are that social enterprise has also arrived and will grow in China.

"We need to give social sector organizations such as social enterprises more power, because we badly need your innovations to counter social deprivation. Social enterprise is the great institutional innovation of our time."

David Cameron, Prime Minister of the United Kingdom of Great Britain and Northern Ireland

TexelEnergie: islander groundedness

The closer you get to TexelEnergie HQ, the more solar panels you see gleaming on the roofs of buildings. Completely absent in Amsterdam, a few in the northern tip of the North Holland province, but as soon as the ferry drops you off on the island of Texel, every house seems to be a paragon of energy awareness.

"Well, that's overstating it a little," says Managing Director Brendan de Graaf. "Our customer base covers only a quarter of the island's population at the moment. So we can still do a lot better."

TexelEnergie is an exceptional power company. Not only because they deliver and produce sustainable energy, but primarily because of the way it is set up: it's a cooperative, which means that it has members instead of shareholders. "TexelEnergie is an initiative by the people, like De Krim, the island's largest holiday park, and TESO, its ferry service. TESO has been around for 105 years, and we have for 5, we started when TESO celebrated its 100-year anniversary," says De Graaf.

Before we continue with TexelEnergie, let's just take a quick look at TESO, *Texels Eigen Stoomboot Onderneming* (Texel's own steamboat company). When this ferry service was founded, there was already a ferry service, which was not to the local population's liking. It was too expensive and provided a poor service. This prompted the locals to start an alternative ferry service themselves, aiming to get the best possible connection to the mainland at the lowest price possible. Seed capital for the non-profit publicly held corporation was raised by islanders contributing 5 guilders each. Or 25, because the wealthy were required to contribute more. Mind you, the amount paid did not affect the level of control, because the rule was: one man, one vote. Today, these shares are worth around 7,000 euros each. What you get for it? Ten free crossings a year. No dividend, as all profits are reinvested. Those profits are enough to buy a new boat once every so many years. The amount of 40 million euros needed for one of those vessels is paid from the cooperative's own capital, not one cent is borrowed from a bank. "And the price of a crossing has even come down over the past few years," says De Graaf. "You do actually get a return on your investment: a delicious cold buffet after the annual shareholders' meeting." He therefore never misses one, also because he has had to solemnly swear to his father that he wouldn't when he was given the share. "It is an honor to be a member of TESO, it awards you a certain status on the island."

And how about TexelEnergie, does that come with similar status? "Well, what can I say? The buffet at our members' meeting is not as abundant: every cent we make, we put back into our company. That said, the sports center we used for our annual meeting is now too small for our 3,100 members. And the theater proved an impractical option. I had to sit on a stage there, simply because that's how the place is set up, but I didn't like that one bit." This is typical of De Graaf, a forty something who combines infectious enthusiasm with the kind of groundedness that is so typical of the islanders. His company is doing well, growing, and raising its profile, and he has already expanded onto the mainland, despite many islanders' fear that it would be a bridge too far: mainlanders can buy their electricity from Texel, or install one of TexelEnergie's solar panels on your roof. Their website offers a handy app that lets you check whether your roof is suited for that. Or you can join the cooperative for 50 euros, following which you have a say in the company's policy — and hopefully will be able to feast on a luscious buffet every year.

But at the end of the day, power is power, even when it is green. So what then is the big difference in comparison to other companies? "The major players in the energy industry try to keep contact with customers to a minimum. We are different, a low-threshold company. Take this morning, when our office was packed. Customers had just received their annual bill and came in with queries. Dealing with those queries takes time, and is perhaps not very efficient, but that's not what it's about. People generally have a negative view of power companies, so before you've done anything you're already up against it public image-wise. We try to create a bond with our customers, also when we grow even further in the future. Because if you have a bond, you will be more lenient toward each other and mean something to each other. That's how you create value for each other. It's hard to express in monetary terms, but that's what it's all about, in my opinion." When we say to him that he really sounds like a social entrepreneur, he almost seems offended. "I am purely business, don't get me wrong. And that is often where I see social initiatives derail: a lot of idealism, a lack of realism, and zero business nous. I prefer to see it this way: when I can help someone, I'll gladly do so. If both sides benefit, even better. Look, we are a not-for-profit organization, but we can make money! What we do with that money, that's another story. The members decide, but I can imagine that if we have something left over under our bottom line, we might spend it on good causes. If we find out the youth home in Den Burg is low on cash, we might give them a couple of solar panels. Something along those lines."

Before he joined a group of people starting a small power company, De Graaf was an installation engineer. "I used to have black hands all day and would wear an overall all the time. Now I find myself writing reports and have secretarial support." He says it as if it's some sort of exotic disease, but it's all a bit of an act, because a few minutes later it turns out De Graaf knows a thing or two. "I know a little bit of everything, like most entrepreneurs. Also about figures, because I have to, because the figures we generate are substantial, we bill hundreds of thousands of euros every month. But I'm aware of my limitations, and that means you have to gather different disciplines around you, such as our finances man, a registered accountant. He does the books in a quarter of the time I would need, while also doing a much better job at it, and enjoying it to boot." This allows De Graaf to focus on other things. On boosting production, for example. TexelEnergie currently procures a large part of the power from third parties. Partially locally, such as wind power from turbines on the island. "One of things we are working on is bio-fermentation. Our aim is to convert the manure and by-products available at farms on Texel into green power, sustainable heat, and digestate, which is fermented manure. But that is far from an easy task, as a lot of time and energy is consumed by obtaining the appropriate permits alone. I don't blame the local authorities though, it is not like a simple permit to cut down a tree, but all very new and certainly not child's play." Procuring and producing power is an unusual combination: most power companies do either, not both. "One is sales, the other technology development. But in my opinion, we must try to do both at the same time, our customers expect that from us, it is one of their reasons for switching to TexelEnergie."

What's De Graaf's take on the Netherlands and sustainable energy? Not positive. "Only four percent of power consumed in the Netherlands is green power, against fifty in Sweden and twenty-four in Germany. The Netherlands has a handicap: it's sitting on huge gas reserves and it is by the sea. The latter makes it easy for us to cool power plants, as a result of which we never really thought about alternative energy sources. We do not reuse waste heat, for example. And we use our gas inefficiently, because we get fifty percent output from it. But hey, it doesn't cost us anything, so it obviously doesn't matter. Although this is about to change soon."

De Graaf gets comfortable, all set to go off on his pet topic. "Did you know that gas from the Slochteren gas field is of inferior quality? And that we will soon be using even worse quality gas? We will soon switch to H gas, which is fine for cooking at home, but a lot of high-grade equipment will not run properly on this gas. Gas will become more expensive, while the oil price will stay steady between eighty and one hundred dollars a barrel. That may not be something we are currently overly worried about, but it is an exorbitantly high price. When the economy picks up again, demand for power will increase, prices will rise even further, and that will inevitably lead to another economic crash. Affordable energy is essential, and we therefore have to look to other sources. The energy market is changing drastically, and fast. Major changes are imminent, and it remains to be seen whether the existing parties can keep operating the way they are. TexelEnergie will not be affected by that, we are lean and mean, we can identify issues and adapt on time."

Our conversation is drawing to a close: we have to catch the ferry back to the mainland and De Graaf has stacks of paperwork on his desk he has to get through — that secretary is certainly not going easy on him.

The initiators of Texel Energie were inspired by the Danish island of Samsø, which is a token of what is possible in renewable energy.

10

The height of entrepreneurship

The future of social enterprise

What we have in mind is a society where fairness, sustain- ability, and solidarity are matters of fact — a society that responds effectively to social challenges. A society where every individual and every group has the freedom to produce social and ecological solutions.

An inclusive society for everyone, also those people who are considered to have "low occupational value." In very simple terms: we want a society of people who want every- one to have a good quality of life, and want to work together in ensuring generations following ours have a better world — or at least not a worse one. This automatically leads to a need to sustainabilize, to treat our planet with care.

In our view, social enterprise plays a key role in that in three important ways.

Firstly, there is the category of *ethical and ecological pioneers*, social enterprises that are showing there is anoth- er way, models that work to create value for everyone. They set an example. Muhammad Yunus came up with a worka- ble microcredit concept, and imitation of his idea has since lifted a lot of people out of poverty. Max Havelaar intro- duced fair trade, and today, thirty years down the line, fair trade products adorn many a supermarket shelf: fair trade is slowly becoming the norm. A company such as Tony's Chocolonely has taken the next step, showing that a supply chain devoid of slavery is possible, and that there are conscientious consumers out there who are willing to pay a premium for that. The major players are bound to copy elements of that modus operandi. Thirty years from now, all cabs will be electric, and the air in our cities a lot cleaner. These cab companies will then have ceased to be social enterprises, and instead be regular cab companies. Taxi Electric shows that it is possible. Specialisterren and Swink are showing that autistic people do have a role to play in our economy, and we hope that many others, from Rabobank to government agencies, decide to deploy a team made up autistic software testers at their IT departments to boost social inclusion of highly qualified autistic people. Social entrepreneurs create new models, from car sharing to complementary monetary systems. This first category of social enterprises is made up of innovative pioneers in a social, ethical, and/or ecological sense.

The second category is that of the authentic social firm, the work integration social enterprise. These are companies that offer opportunities to people with disabilities, people who without very specific facilities would be sidelined, companies such as Landzijde's care farms. The fact that they create economic value makes them more than mere care providers. They provide jobs, not just something to do during the day, even though the work these employees do does not stretch to full recovery of the boss' costs. That is why we classed Specialisterren in the first category, because there are many people who are currently considered to have "low occupational value," but who have the capacity to do as good a job as anyone, provided the company can accommodate their specific needs. The latter is precisely where a competency of social enterprises lies, as they are able to create such a work environment. But that does not go for everyone, as there will always be people who cannot reach that level of productivity due to psychological or physical circumstances. Care is also needed.

The third main category is that of community enterprises: local companies and residents' collectives that, alongside their normal business operations providing jobs and local economy, play a role in the development of local ties and social cohesion, and hence fulfill a natural human need.

Best practices

Social entrepreneurs have a lot to offer. Barroso expressed the expectation that in the near future the social economy will be 10 percent of the economy, where social enterprises are the key. That's a fine figure, an appealing put-a-man-on-the-moon goal, but what would be even more interesting is when the impact of social enterprises is felt beyond their own industry, which would be the case when "regular" companies start increasingly adopting social entrepreneurs' way of thinking. That would lead to the increased scale that is needed to achieve major and lasting social change. Some services, such as community enterprises focused on cohesion or companies with large numbers of occupationally-impaired employees, will remain exclusively within specialist social enterprises, albeit that their number will swell.

Growth in the number of social enterprises does, of course, not mean that we will never list companies ever again, but it does mean that a large number of companies may just question the fulfillment obtained from maximizing shareholder value, and think twice about a stock market launch. Our hope is that they will assume a more long-term focus when setting objectives, and that they will change the way they approach their staff, resources, and governance model.

An important step toward more social enterprises is awareness and recognition of the phenomenon and its impact; that's when opportunities will arise. Schools and universities can play a big part here. They could train talent, perhaps even from high school. Not only through a "social enterprise" module, but an entire course, as already offered by Harvard, Stanford, and INSEAD, or even a complete MBA program, like the Social Entrepreneurship MBA offered by Oxford University's Saïd Business School. Business schools could teach students how to use entrepreneurial skills to make the world a better place, and cultural and social studies programs at the higher vocational education level could include classes on how to approach social goals from a business perspective. Research at the higher education level will also help for studying and sharing best practices.

We also need role models. Social entrepreneurship should not be seen as a soft form of entrepreneurship, but instead as the ivy league of entrepreneurship. After all, taking care of a successful company's dual bottom line requires top-class entrepreneurs.

There is still so much work to do, and so much for us to contribute to the growth of the social enterprise sector. That is what we set out to show through this book. Whether you are a policymaker, consumer, or investor, we can do it together. It's also a modern thing, the tide is in our favor, because whether you call it blue economy, circular economy, or sharing economy, there is a real shift ongoing in our society, a shift toward a new way of value creation. We hope this shift carries through, becomes mainstream, and is embraced by an ever greater part of society.

WakaWaka: light in the darkness

WakaWaka, not to be confused with Shakira's hit song of the same name, means "shine" in Swahili and that is exactly what these lamps do. Charge the WakaWaka Light in the, not even very bright, sunshine for eight hours, and you've got sixteen hours of light. Dual benefits: not only for you, but also for people in Africa and Asia who are currently without light in the evening, for children who cannot do their homework or only amid the hazardous fumes of a kerosene lamp, or for women who have to walk unsafe dark streets. The latest invention is WakaWaka Power, a lightweight chargeable battery, highly innovative, that can charge your cell phone or iPad. For every WakaWaka Power Pack sold, one Haitian citizen, who is still homeless following the devastating natural disasters in the recent past, will receive a lamp.

10 percent of revenue generated through lamp sales in the West goes to the WakaWaka Foundation, which subsequently sees to it that lamps are available in Zambia, Vietnam, or South Africa. But not even the poorest people get the lamp for free: the idea behind that is that when you pay for something, you will take better care of it. WakaWaka has set out to equip 1.5 billion people in the Third World with sustainable and affordable light. WakaWaka Light is meanwhile used all over the globe, has won many a prestigious award, and has some very famous fans, ranging from Bill Clinton to Brad Pitt.

WakaWaka is the brainchild of Maurits Groen, who has been living up to his last name for many years ("groen" is Dutch for "green"): he got Al Gore to speak at an event in the Netherlands, tried to make the soccer world cup in South Africa a carbon-neutral event, and keeps moving up *Trouw* newspaper's sustainability chart.

WakaWaka Power was bankrolled through a crowdfunding campaign on Kickstarter and Oneplanetcrowd. It took only a few days to raise the required seed capital of 100,000 euros.

WakaWaka's success has meanwhile attracted the attention of major corporations, who initially questioned the lamp's financial feasibility, as most potential customers are extremely poor and not hooked up to the power grid. Maurits is a true social entrepreneur, who just wanted to make this lamp happen, not for its financial potential, but because it will make the lives of 1.5 billion people a lot better. That's what counts.

How to start a company that will help make the world a better place

Step 1. What are you passionate about?
What drives you? Which social problem do you want to solve? Do you want to help disadvantaged people get a job, fight poverty, or tackle an environmental issue? A social entrepreneur wants to do business to better the world.

Step 2. What do you have to offer?
Business is not simple, it takes guts and a willingness to take risk. Self-reflection is one of the most important initial steps. Do you have the commitment and perseverance? Which competencies do you possess and are you able to get others excited about your idea and build a team? Starting a business will take a lot of hard work!

Step 3. What is your business idea and your theory of change?
What is your business idea and how will it help solve the social problem you have identified? Not all problems lend themselves to the social enterprise model. Some problems call for a political solution or should be taken up by a charity.

A social enterprise only has a chance of succeeding when the business model is clear and well thought out, when it has a clear underlying theory of change.

Step 4. The business plan

An old-fashioned business plan may prove helpful, albeit one based on social principles and with a clear mission and a well-positioned product or service. Your business plan must contain a systematic translation of all your ideas about your enterprise into actions that can be implemented in practice. Carefully consider your target group: who are your customers, and will they pay a competitive price for the experience you are offering? Think about measuring results: what does your social impact look like, and how will you quantify it? And then there is the financial side: how much money do you need?

Step 5. A team that can be successful

Social entrepreneurship is a team sport. Who will you need to make this a success? Which competencies do you need and how do get them on board? Are you capable of building a team of people who can get the company on its feet in the start-up phase? That also includes financial backers, they are part of the team. Which financiers and business partners would fit your model? Find partners who support your mission. They should preferably not only invest money, but also expertise or provide access to a network. Make all the contacts you need during this stage.

Step 6. Validation and financing

In this phase, the last of the "homework" phases, it is important to also look at others; who is already active in the market, and what are they doing? Social entrepreneurs like to share their experiences. Make contact and make sure you learn from the successes and failures of others. Approach experts, have them review your plan, ask for feedback. Being new and innovative is nice, but not the overriding aim. It's about the impact you achieve. The initial phase is difficult enough as it is, so try to keep to the beaten track wherever possible. This phase will have to persuade prospective financial backers to take the plunge. Some business concepts can start small without extensive resources, and if that is possible in your case, you should do so, because that's how you learn the most.

Step 7. Start

This is when you get started — like any other company. Get registered, shape your product or service, and then you can start selling. At this stage, it's ok to push your social goals to the background to make sure your company takes off, to post your first successes, and eventually start breaking even. As soon as you do, you will have created a basis from which to create real value and be truly meaningful.

What's next?

If you want to grow, increase your impact, you will face yet more challenges. In attracting new capital, for example. And, which is often even trickier, in finding new people with the skills required to run a larger company, who have different professional competencies. As in step 2, you will have to ask yourself whether you are the right person to lead the company into the next phase. Whether you possess the required management skills and whether you would actually enjoy it. If impact comes first, you have to do whatever it takes to achieve that impact, and that often means the initiator has to morph into different roles in the different stages of the process.

Acknowledgments

158   There are many people we would like to thank for contributing to this book, it is with them that we share the mission of raising awareness to social entrepreneurship across the world.

Our co-creators
Co-author Mark Schalekamp, publisher Wardy Poelstra, and translator Erwin Postma.

Our sources of inspiration and their teams
Sjoerd van der Maaden, Ronald van Vliet, Boudewijn Poelmann, Sandra Ballij, Maurits Groen, Bas van Abel, Willem van Rijn, Sarriel Taus, Brendan de Graaf, Ruud Zandvliet, Edvard Hendriksen, Patrick Anthonissen, Mathijs Huis in 't Veld, Rob van den Dool, Stephan Zeijlemaker, Quirijn Bolle, Henk Jan Beltman, Teun van de Keuken, Jos de Blok, Frank van Beuningen, Margaret van Beuningen, Katja Schuurman, Willem des Tombe, Jaap Hoek Spaans, Marieke Hart, Bart-Jan Krouwel, Peter Blom, Henry Mentink, and all volunteers and members of Social Enterprise NL.

Our reviewers
Ivo Brautigam, Marian Lambert, Annelies Weijschede, Dylan Selvig, Ingmar Schuster, and Selma Steenhuisen, who never let up in keeping us focused.

Our supporters

Our work is largely made possible by a number of wonderful partners; PwC, ABN AMRO, CMS Lawfirms, Cordaid, Anton Jurgens Fonds and Stichting DOEN. Our special thanks go out to Reineke Schermer, Manon Klein, Judith Lingeman, Frans Jurgens, Tineke Kemp, Tera Terpstra, Simone Filippini, Wouter van Tongeren, Eveline Maas, Richard Kooloos, Andius Teijgeler, Peter van Mierlo, Robert van der Laan, Sandra Hazenberg, Wineke Haagsma, Dolf Segaar, Katja van Kranenburg, and Robert Carsouw for their support and engaging collaboration.

Our backbone

Our terrific team: Nina Koopman, Arine van Heeswijk, Stefan Panhuijsen, Marijt Regts, and Meike Zwaan! And above all our life companions: Wieneke, Rob, Bodhi, Dante, Elsa, and Chilli.

About Willemijn Verloop

As a historian, young activist, and founder of the War Child charity, I was driven by a desire to learn from the history of our world in helping create a fairer future; putting up with injustice is simply not in my nature. Over the fifteen years I headed up War Child, I experienced up close that even the darkest places on earth lend themselves to the creation of something positive.

What has occupied my mind since my time at War Child is the question of how to make the most effective contribution to society. What will lead to strong and sustainable development? I remember the day I first heard about Muhammad Yunus, the man behind Grameen Bank, a thoroughbred social entrepreneur. His approach and that of entrepreneurs like him inspires me tremendously, mainly because the social enterprise model paves the way for both efficiency and innovation — which is not always the case in development aid. Social entrepreneurs engage with the market, which forces are now, after several years of being slated as perverse, proving fruitful for social entrepreneurs, forcing them toward effectiveness and innovation, and helping them achieve their social objective.

Aforementioned innovation, together with entrepreneurs' independence, is crucial in the development of new and structural solutions to social problems in the world. Awareness of the power and potential of social entrepreneurs is still largely lacking in the Netherlands, so I found out, and I wanted to know why. Together with a top-class team from McKinsey & Company, I ran a study into this at the end of 2011.* The main conclusion we drew was that the Netherlands brims with opportunities for a strong social enterprise industry.

There's work to be done, I thought. So here we are, my new challenge, which I have taken up together with Mark Hillen and a fine team of collaborators. Aside from that, I'm also active in various (social) organizations and in 2014 I founded Social Impact Ventures NL, an investment management organization that helps Netherlands-based social enterprises realize their growth ambitions.

P.S. Yumeko's Rob van den Dool is my favorite social entrepreneur, by far. I like him so much that we've been together for over 20 years!

* Verloop & McKinsey, 'Opportunities for the Dutch Social Enterprise Sector', 2011

About Mark Hillen

It may be hard to believe, but when I studied economics in college that was still considered one of the social sciences. As concepts, wealth and well-being were on a par. In fact, the latter actually outweighed the former. This laid the foundations for my present motives.

I wanted to develop as a professional, see the world, and so I joined a management consultancy. Back in 1985, the company that now goes by the name of Accenture was a firm of fifty employees in the Netherlands. I was posted at major international corporations. When I left in 2007, having attained Managing Partner status, Accenture was a listed company with 180,000 employees across the globe.

Nothing but success. But what is success? These corporations are primarily focused on maximizing shareholder value, because the shareholders are the owners and their word is law. I started researching how meaningful that actually is. The limitations of this model came poignantly to the fore in an analysis of the pharmaceutical industry around the year 2000.

In those days, I would travel to Africa every year, to take a vacation and to take part in projects in Tanzania and Namibia. I witnessed the extremes of having a lot and having very little. Pharmaceutical manufacturers made over 18 cents profit on each dollar of revenue, but they did not develop medicine to combat poverty-related diseases, such as typhoid and cholera. Financially unattractive, because the target group would be patients with little resources. That may make perfect business sense, but it doesn't feel right.

On my travels, I also saw that people there are often no less happy than people over here. Disease and dire poverty lead to unhappiness, but money alone evidently does not bring happiness either.

The time had come for me to devote my energy to matters that are eventually far more important than money. I got involved in social initiatives, as a consultant and investor, and also as the co-founder of Social Enterprise Lab and *Wekomenerwel* (refer to page 124). As I searched for new ways, I met Willemijn Verloop. Our ideas matched and we have the same optimism and drive, coupled with highly complementary expertise and skills. The pieces of the jigsaw puzzle fell into place. Our efforts are devoted to a meaningful goal, with pleasure. And this does feel right.

Index

Printed in the USA
CPSIA information can be obtained
at www.ICGtesting.com
LVHW092116261124
797681LV00002B/214